TIME AND TIME AGAIN

Edited by

Becki Mee

First published in Great Britain in 2000 by
POETRY NOW
Remus House,
Coltsfoot Drive,
Woodston,
Peterborough, PE2 9JX
Telephone (01733) 898101
Fax (01733) 313524

All Rights Reserved

Copyright Contributors 2000

HB ISBN 0 75430 935 5
SB ISBN 0 75430 936 3

FOREWORD

Although we are a nation of poets we are accused of not reading poetry, or buying poetry books. After many years of listening to the incessant gripes of poetry publishers, I can only assume that the books they publish, in general, are books that most people do not want to read.

Poetry should not be obscure, introverted, and as cryptic as a crossword puzzle: it is the poet's duty to reach out and embrace the world.

The world owes the poet nothing and we should not be expected to dig and delve into a rambling discourse searching for some inner meaning.

The reason we write poetry (and almost all of us do) is because we want to communicate: an ideal; an idea; or a specific feeling. Poetry is as essential in communication, as a letter; a radio; a telephone, and the main criterion for selecting the poems in this anthology is very simple: they communicate.

CONTENTS

Kersey In July	Richard Maslen	1
Allotment	Larry Crehan	2
Tribute To A Mother	Joyce W Parsons	3
Swallows	Pam Dutton	4
Last Week The Wind	J Wilde	5
Coffee	Hazel Cooper	6
My Mother's Grave	Marion Roberts	7
Autumn	A Horton	8
To My Grandson	R G Baker	9
Memories	Alice Ackland	10
A Fisherman's Lament	Jean Reynolds	11
Front To Back	Sian Jenkins	12
Dark Days Approaching	Kim Montia	13
To Maddie	Doris Hughes	14
A Pleasant Sunday Afternoon Trip In January To Felixstowe	Adrian Bullard	15
The Tapestry Of Love	T Flower	16
Autumn Leaves	V Rowlands	17
Seasons	D Robshaw	18
Seasons Of Life	Mary Howard	19
A Day In The Nursery	Winifred Forster	20
Solar Eclipse Norfolk 11.8.99	Wendy Thrower	21
Nights	Mary Parslow	22
Taking Down The Big Breakwater	Andria J Cooke	23
God Bless My Angel	Annie Clode	24
Me	Mary Elizabeth Percy-Burns	25
Eve Of The Millennium - Remembrance Sunday 1999	Rose Dempsey	26
The Sheepdog	Sarah Latos	27
A Tree	Kayleigh Hardy	28
Mrs Who?	David H Mead	29
I'll Be There	Michelle Dunnett	30
Time/Space	Vera Boyle	31

Title	Author	Page
Choosing You	Nina Thomas	32
Mother	Vikki Smith	33
Techno Phobia	Sally Vale	34
Silverdene Cottage	L Pigrome	35
Please Make It Soon	V J Aldridge	36
Maitreya, World Teacher	Ursula Johnson	37
The Shoe Cupboard	Myrtle Elden	38
Research	Doug McGhee	39
The Hall Of Records	Matt Annis	40
Diss	B Scales	41
My Granny's Back Garden	Sylvia Southgate	42
Ever Near	Rev Lew Park	43
Untitled	Amy Phillips	44
A Period In Time	Sheralee Le-Gros	45
The Rock Pool	Tricia Cuming	46
Hunstanton	Leslie Moate	47
Reflections	Margaret Adams	48
Yesteryear - Today - Tomorrow	Mervyn A Whitmore	49
Millennium Bug Alert!	Allison D Fowles	50
For Keith	Donna	51
Heavenly Justice	Madge H Paul	52
Love	Christina Miller	54
Tears	David D Bourne	55
For Me	Sue Kitson	56
Moving Again!	Linda Roberts	57
Untitled	Mary Colquhoun	58
The Boy's Exams	Tricia Porter	59
The Grass Is Always Greener	Mick Nash	60
The Snail And The Fly	Lisa Bristow	61
Globes Of Creativity	Daniel North	62
The Rock	P W Pidgeon	63
The Dreamland Horse	Maxine Kaye	64
Jasmine	David Phillip Thomas	65
Deforestation	Darren Challis	66
A Walk In The Park	N Carruthers	67
Hold Your Kitten	Keith L Powell	68

Friend Or Foe	Audrey Williams	69
Autumn Lullaby	Grace Longman	70
Turmoil	Luke Thomas	71
Invitation To Love	Gerard Oxley	72
Fire!	Karen Brooke	73
Why?	B Scotney	74
Hewn From Clouds	Daphne Foreman	75
Red Alert	T A Napper	76
Fickle	P Tatley	77
Dawn	Matt Deacon	78
Hide And Seek	Deanna L Dixon	79
Just One Wish	Violet M Corlett	80
Wrapping Gran	C Lancaster	81
Vacuum	M R Mackinnon-Pattison	82
The Elements	Joan May Wills	83
Why Weepest Thou?	Ailsa Keen	84
A Patient's Eye View	Jill Ives	85
Spring In The Air	J W Holmes	86
A Special Thanks To All The Nurses Everywhere!	Tony W Rylatt	87
Through The Ages	Nancy Owen	88
Thinking Of Clouds	John Aldred	89
An Island Of Dreams	Betsey Prose	90
Jack Frost	Kathryn J Hayward	91
Smoke Control Order	Florence Taylor	92
Eerie	Charles Butler	93
Three Lives	Alfa	94
Late Autumn	Josephine Moreau	95
A Time To Run	Roy McCadden	96
The Sadists	B Colebourn	97
Love	Geraldine Ward	98
Ante Millennium	Lisa Wolfe	99
No More Mr Nice Guy	Tony Sheldon	100
Perseverance	Barbara Hampson	101
Nouveau Riche (Noo-Voh Reesh) Queen: Know What I Mean?	Jackie Docherty	102

Title	Author	Page
Destiny	J W Anderton	104
Came The Rain	R Smith	105
Isolation?	Muriel Berry	106
Listen To Me	Deirdre Armes Smith	107
Seven	Marlene Allen	108
The Fog	Susan Jenkinson	109
Getty'sburgh	Dennis F Tye	110
Spring	Heather Aspinall	111
To A Swift	Eddie Sykes	112
The Love Within	Jack Ryan	113
Toby	Judy Buxton	114
Why Me?	Jim Preston	116
A Pleasing Power	H Cotterill	117
PMS	Mandy Parker	118
Swinton Fields	R E Fairclough	120
Searching	Joyce Brown	121
Come My Love	Carole H Sexton	122
Mystery Of Space	Elizabeth A Wilkinson	123
Distress! (Or, The Lifeboat)	J Millington	124
Butterfly Heart	Jane Solan-Robertson	126
Feathered Friends?	Angela Pritchard	127
My Little House	P Tattersall	128
Lost Child	Patricia Brown	129
Changing Seasons	Marion Pollitt	130
The Seasons	Bunty Yates Aldred	131
Who Am I?	Holly Stewart	132
A Prayer For The New Millennium	Yolande Hall	133
Nu-Speak	Elizabeth Rapley	134
Neighbours 'R' Hell	Michael Bellerby	135
Small Again	Paula Morris	136
The Beauty Of The Morning	Julie Gaskell	137
Early Spring	Mavis Preston-Riley	138
Susie	Sylvia D Saunders	139
He Loves Me Really	Linda Woodhouse	140
The Dilemma	Bill Johnson	141

Title	Author	Page
Nether Bower	G E Sowerby	142
The Freedom Of Solitude	Ray Pilling	143
Lara	Seth Wilkins	144
Time Slips By	Mighty Mouse	145
Stones	Frances Etheridge	146
Loss	Lily Jeffries	148
My Memory	Edna A M Cattermole	149
The Faces Of Niagara	David Bridgewater	150
Fighting Alone	Angela Taylor	152
Clouds	C A Browne	153
Mr Right	Mary Andersen	154
The Battle	Adam Kennedy	155
It's So Quiet...	Julie Ann Garritty	156
The Woodsman	Sarah Kaye Martin	157
My Child Quietly Sleeps	Simon Cardy	158
Albert The Elf	S M Rooney	159
Mother	Jock Milne	160
Sub Conscience	Brenda Nicholson	161
Shadows	Hazel Wellings	162
Fear Rubs My Senses	Martin Howard	163
Freedom To Roam	Ian Barton	164
The New Millennium	Robert Baslington	165
Kirstie's Song	Sharon Gardner	166
Bedsit land	Donna M Holt	167
Castle Deceased	D J Holt	168
Forest Fruits	David Charles	169
On Reflection	Kathleen Leigh	170
For Carlo The Cavalier	David F Upson	171
Pig Wiggy	Olwyn Kershaw	172
Love Is In The Air 2000	Brenda R Matthews	173
A Poem/Song About Insomnia	Anthony Cohen	174
The Tall Ships	D H Taylor	175
E Frow 1906-1997	H Livesey	176
My First Grandchild	Richard Wallbank	177
Shuttle Scuttle	Roy Gordon	178
Silence	Carole Anne Weaver	179

My Misunderstood Husband	Helen McEvoy	180
Ageless	C Allison	181
Lost Friends	Joseph Yates	182
Alec Anonymous	Jake	183
The Covering Letter	Dale Overton	184
Sparkle And Glow	F Williamson	185
Our County	Joan Smith	186
Life's Pathway	Lynda Banks	188
The Morning Walk	Anne Patricia Jones	189
Totally Temperance	Francis Arthur Rawlinson	190
Sundays On Lady Street	Paul Kelly	191
The Raging Sea	Eddie Preston	192

KERSEY IN JULY

Is this the rapture?
This silence on a summer's day?
Houses smothered in hollyhock and mallow,
A coloured profusion pouring over garden walls,
The ford alive with ducks and small birds.
An absence of people.
Only ourselves,
Observers of this timeless place.

Worn steps draw us upwards
And in the heat,
Turning at the top,
England lies open to the sky.
Cows, meadows, cornfields
All hazed in the sun.

This is England's core.
No sound in the village below,
Even the bees are still.
My eyes blur with tears,
The land outspread
Under a blue and perfect
Heaven.

Richard Maslen

Allotment

And the lane's smell winding
Down the old boy's patch
By the barrow-load manure slicked.

Carrot fingers probing holes for veg
Picked nuts to screw for seed,
For rent, for kids' boots, for what we ate.

Railings leaned back from rhubarb
Below the banked line thundering steel,
Showering cinder on the cabbage.

And a cigarette rolled, hanging shag
By the shed on a bucket;
And his dirt-dry hands on the haft.

Larry Crehan

TRIBUTE TO A MOTHER

My heart is tinged with sadness
now I know that you are gone
silent tears will always flow
forever, on and on.

Please take care of my mum Lord
please be gentle and kind
I loved her so much
she was hard to find.

I had a mum who didn't care
a father who was never there
but you and Pop gave me such hope
you gave me strength, to help me cope.

I grew so steadily in your tender care
because I knew you were always there
I learned so much in my tender years
you always made sure I was free from sadness and tears.

Soon I shall leave this house that was home
my thoughts and memories ever to roam
we shared so much laughter, we had so much fun
what shall I do Mum, now you are gone.

With kindness of friends and neighbours who cared
troubles were halved and troubles were shared
they helped me so much, far beyond measure
but alas, now Mum I have only memories to treasure.

Joyce W Parsons

SWALLOWS

High in the sky
The swallows fly,
Gliding on arrow-like wings.
Swift and fleet
Each other they meet
Happy with beautiful things.

Summery days
Clear blue skyways.
Enjoying these they are
Gaining the strength
For the graphic event
When they travel to lands afar.

Beautiful things
On feathery wings
No noise and quarrelsome sounds.
Gliding along
The summer's one song.
Pleasure and beauty abounds.

Pam Dutton

LAST WEEK THE WIND

Last week the wind turned round
And bore down upon our town
The streets filled with whipping leaves
And people leaning blindly

Nature's loose bits came tumbling down
To be carried off beyond our grasp
A teacher I know tried to kill himself
In a howling gale of his own design

A baby died in the house next door
They cried all night through the bedroom walls
Louder than the wind and longer than the dark
My wife lay wide-eyed, silent

All that week we snarled and swore
And walked on broken glass
All men swallowed their bitter grief
The women bit their pain in half

And when the wind has left us scattered
Rolled itself up and barged away
Our heads hesitated to lift again
And a silence welled up from every dust-clogged drain

J Wilde

COFFEE

To wake to the smell of it
To drink and read
Brightens the day's prospects enormously
It has such special qualities.

When meeting friends and family
In a restaurant filled with people chatting
To savour the superb taste of it
Is something to be remembered.

Shopping is not the same without it
Lunch too needs its taste
An evening meal is supported by it
So the day goes by.

Which blend to buy becomes confusing
Colours too are different
Packages appealing or drab
And this affects our choice.

Coffee is a reason for listening
It's a pleasure nothing can rival
An opportunity to watch people
And can only be recommended.

Hazel Cooper

My Mother's Grave

The leaves have fallen
on my mother's grave
the cross battered by the wind
whose greedy arms
ravaged the tall chrysanthemums.

There I stood again
embracing the sullen darkness
not a sound
other than nature's voice
on the pensive night of All Souls.

I cannot speak to you
you cannot laugh with me
we share our tears no longer
nor the touch of hand and mind
our power vanished, your spirit gone.

I'm left alone and sad
your gentle, guiding voice,
your smile now etched in sleep.
I want to move the earth
and see your face once more
and lie beside you, facing heaven.

Marion Roberts

Autumn

The gentle breeze that plucks the leaf
And floats it softly down to earth,
The russet scene confirms belief
That nature once more gives its birth
To autumn.

The trees stand out against the sky
But winter has not gripped them yet,
Their golden tints must catch the eye
Must capture hues and colours set
For autumn.

The carpet spreads throughout the wood
From palest gold to deepest brown
And as I looked I understood
Why nature surely has its crown
In autumn.

A Horton

To My Grandson

God's sweet child in earth's disguise,
Oh little angel in my eyes,
Drenched in purity,
With glory clinging from afar,
Adorned with heavenly light, you are
A soul so dear to me.

For three summers and two winters long,
The world has heard the glorious song
Of a precious little boy,
Of innocence and simplicity,
Dazzling naiveté,
Laughter, love and joy.

Ignorant of hate or sin,
With your cheeky impish grin,
You are a part of me
And through the pleasure that you give,
You will forever laugh and live
Within the heart of me.

May your life float gently as the breeze,
That murmurs softly through the trees
And fragrant summer flowers,
Alive to all the wondrous sights,
Sounds and smells and sweet delights
In sunshine, shade and showers.

Dear infant without blot or stain,
I pray this brilliance shall remain
Until your race is run,
And that you will rarely see
Dark clouds of cold adversity
To shade you from the sun.

R G Baker

MEMORIES

Remember the excitement
The first time you saw his face,
How you floated high on fluffy clouds
In that first sweet embrace.

Remember the excitement
Of that first shy tender kiss,
And how you wished forever,
There'd be memories like this.

Remember the excitement
When the next date would arrive,
He'd pick you up, a drink, a meal,
A walk or just a drive.

Remember the excitement
Getting ready just to please,
He'd smile with admiration,
Give you compliments and tease.

Remember the excitement
Feeling safe when he's around,
The emotional security
In this new love you've found.

Remember the excitement
Listen well to one who knows,
For if this love's your true love,
This excitement, daily, grows.

Alice Ackland

A Fisherman's Lament

Keep the fire burning Florence
I will be with you by and by,
Keep the kettle boiling Florence
'Til we are together, you and I.
The waves are crashing all about us
Fierce and violent blows the storm
Poke the embers into life now
How long 'til I be dry and warm?
Should it not go in my favour
And fate decrees that I should die,
Do not weep now for me Florence
But mourn me with your head held high.
Florence, I feel the storm abating,
I can see the Northern Star,
Keep your passion fiery Florence
Soon I will join you where you are.

Jean Reynolds

Front To Back

Imagine a world where the sky is green
The grass is blue, the sewers clean
The fish can fly, the birds can swim
Trousers for her, a skirt for him
Dogs don't woof; they miaow like a cat
Imagine that!
Wear your shoes on your hands, your gloves on your feet
While you're walking down the street
With your feet in the air, on your head you are sat
Imagine that!
The moon shines in the day, the sun shines at night
But we still seem to get enough light
Couch potatoes are slim, dancers are fat
Imagine that!
The world has gone bonkers
Everyone's mad
At funerals you're happy at weddings you're sad
You wear knickers on your head; there's' no need for a hat
Imagine that!

Sian Jenkins (11)

DARK DAYS APPROACHING

Dark days, they are approaching
Each one at the speed of light
And snipers are positioned
Have their targets in their sights

Minutes tick on steadily
And hours gallop by
An end has come to talking
Watch the dove, how fast she flies

The shards of an agreement
Lay on Stormont's steps, a mess
The joint work of a British
And a Unionist address

The cease-fire is over
Hear the message of the guns
A free united Ireland
Is the aim of Erin's sons.

Kim Montia

TO MADDIE

Johnathan Joe
Is a cat that I know
And he's full of surprises.
Through the cat flap
He'll jump on your lap
And bring you birds 'n' mices!
He loves Miss Maddie
'Cos she's not faddy
But strokes and tickles his nose.
She'll put down his food
As long as he's good,
Then play and wiggle her toes.

Oh Johnathan Joe
I *love* you so -
Miaow, miaow, miaow!

Doris Hughes

A Pleasant Sunday Afternoon Trip in January to Felixstowe

The weather is very unpredictable at this time of year
and today is a fine example.
The journey to Felixstowe consisted of bright sunshine
and light rain and you would think we were in April already.
To think this morning I awoke with frost and ice all around!

I sat on the beach with a snack, which included soup
and some Christmas goodies, whilst listening to the waves
and feeling the light salted breeze on my face.

There was a lot of movement today, people strolling along the
promenade, fishermen waiting for their 'catch of the day' and
boats entering and leaving the port.

I used my foot to write 'Adi' in the sand, but within hours
the sea would have washed it away with its strong nightly waves
and, now safely at home, I sit tucked up in the warm
knowing that I was there today.

Adrian Bullard

THE TAPESTRY OF LOVE

How may I fathom his love for me:
or plumb the depths of my love for him?
When husband and lover and father
and child, he is all-in-all to me?

Woven we were, when first we met
into a single tapestry: with he the
warp and I the weft. How could I live
without my love, when he is all to me?

We are one tapestry, he and I:
woven of the bright hues of love,
and the dull colours of mundane life.
The radiant hues of our happy times
cheek by jowl with the black of strife.

Enmeshed as I am in the toils of love:
bound by unbreakable gossamer threads,
the warmth of his love binds me fast:
entraps me yet sets me free.

If ever the flame of his love for me
should flicker away and die,
how may I gather the sundered threads of life?
For the tapestry may not ever survive
when warp is cruelly torn from weft.

How could I repair the fabric of life
without the strong warp of his love,
on which to weave once more what once I had?
The tapestry of love.

T Flower

AUTUMN LEAVES

Gazing
on rare precious jewels,
autumn leaves,
crowning glory
of the changing season,
summer radiance
fading into autumn mists,
each glow of red and gold,
russet and yellow
a bright spark of hope.

V Rowlands

SEASONS

We say goodbye to summer,
It has so quickly passed,
The long hot days, the sultry nights
We knew they couldn't last.
To have the joys of summer
That would last the whole year through,
Would be the wish of most of us,
But this I say to you.
When winter comes and fires are lit
And friends they come to call
To enjoy an evening's partying
With fun for one and all,
The summer's soon forgotten
In an atmosphere of leisure
We find the nights of winter
Can also give us pleasure.
It isn't hard to realise
There really is a reason
For the pleasures and the drawbacks
To each and every season.

D Robshaw

SEASONS OF LIFE

Why should it be? What are the reasons
For travelling through all of *life's* seasons?
Enjoying the spring and learning that showers
Prepare us for summer - the rain and the flowers.
We brave autumn's approach with a quick backward glance
Thank God we've been spared and given the chance
To enjoy at long last, the warmth of *September*
The bright vibrant colourful *October, November*.
Only to find at the end of the trail
Suddenly we have become very frail.
We're weary, we're fragile, beginning to wane;
But take heart in the *seasons* -
Spring does come again!

Mary Howard

A DAY IN THE NURSERY

We come at nine, our spirits high,
Hats and coats, off they fly
The boys and girls start to play
'Til all at once they're heard to say -
'The toilet please to spend a penny'

So through we trail - oh so many!
Milk and biscuits eat with pleasure
Sweets and bananas without measure.
Out to play, don hats and coats,
Shoes and scarves, caps and boots.
Sand tray full, sand tray emptying -
Not to waste it, oh, so tempting.

In to lunch - wash those hands
Sit at table - great demands.
Now say grace, then sweep the floor,
Lost your chance to ask for more.

Settle down to television, heave a sigh
For peace and quiet and make the most of those few minutes
'Cause any time there'll be a riot.
Plasticine and pastry, painting - take your pick,
Make a gorgeous mess - clear it up - right quick.
Half past two - what a blessing
Time to dress - no more messing,
Sweep and tidy, turn off stoves,
Pile the chairs - no more moves
Smile at parents, say '*Yes* they're good'
Tongue in cheek and hit the road.

Winifred Forster

SOLAR ECLIPSE NORFOLK 11.8.99

Stillness:
Planet stops its breath.
Clouds - gun - metal - grey
hang heavily around a chill of blue.

Sun half crescent
fights for rights.
Silent twilight falls.

Un-natural - dark
waits for old endings.

Glancing towards the light,
fearing its brilliance blinds,
curiosity compels.

Sudden cool winds blow us around
the back of the century,
ushering new days.

Thoughtful birds hesitantly sing.
Normal service is being resumed.

Wendy Thrower

NIGHTS

Night is so daunting
Lights and shadows so haunting
One hour takes at least five to pass
How long will this night last.

Daylight dawns oh so bright
Your heart though is filled with fright
Loneliness fades with the dark
As the living make their mark

You have endured another night's long
Lonely hours

But where are the flowers?

Mary Parslow

TAKING DOWN THE BIG BREAKWATER

Men built you up, they made you proud and strong,
A queen among your peers. They raised you higher
And dug you deep, in pride of place, so long
Ago, then named you for the patron squire.
They must have laboured hard to set you straight,
To hoist your bars and stays amid the tide.
Then generations swarmed about your great
Foot-posts, landmark and best of beaches' bride.
But then you seemed to shrink, salt-cracked and bleached
To silver-grey, still regal but like bones.
A hundred years of pounding never breached,
But water wore you thin and waves of stones
Have risen round. Dismantled in a day
Forever, felled unmourned, you pass away.

Andria J Cooke

GOD BLESS MY ANGEL

I miss you so much now you
have gone to sleep
I miss your sweet face
I want to weep

I miss holding your hand
to guide me the right way
I miss talking to you
when I am far away

I take comfort in knowing
you are watching over us all,
to keep us safe
so we will not fall
and help us all to stand tall

Love is forever my precious one.
The blue skies will come and so will the sun.

God bless Mummy

                Annie xxx

Annie Clode

ME

Today was like
Mining gold
I felt good
And 'right on'
And really, really
Together,
Flying, flying
Through hours
Feeling jewels
Encrusted on my
Wings
Dazzling everybody.
I am beginning to fly on my own;
Perhaps tomorrow
I will try some
Acrobatics if the
Jewels don't come
Unstuck of course!

Mary Elizabeth Percy-Burns

EVE OF THE MILLENNIUM - REMEMBRANCE SUNDAY 1999

As we reach the eve of the new millennium,
so must we remember those who gave their lives in this,
the last century of the old;
their hope,
that we might have a better life,
in a peaceful world -
we owe them this.
As we look around,
there is an apathy, a canker among us.
Violence rears its head daily,
in words, thoughts and deeds and yet
there are those whose smile will warm the coldest morning
and children,
in whose innocence is our hope for the future.
And here, too, also walk angels,
selfless in their desire, their wish to help others,
often anonymous and un-thanked.
As we watch the pomp and glory of the massed bands,
the sea of uniforms marching in unison
to the raucous applause of the crowd,
let hearts and minds be opened
to the reality of the why.
Why they are there and we watch.
Sons and brothers, most; husbands and fathers, some.
Lost. Forever.
Memories only in the hearts of those who loved them.
As the poppy petals fall . . . silence.
Our respect. We knew them not,
yet owe them - one and all.

14th November 1999.

Rose Dempsey

THE SHEEPDOG

Black and white races across the green,
joining the white dots into an
undulating woollen sea.
Moving left then right,
effortless, silent.

Sarah Latos

A Tree

I saw a tree all torn and tattered,
Twigs scattered all over the place,
All bare by the coldness of the autumn wind,
But in the spring in all its glory,
Glistening and gleaming in the sunshine.

Winter comes so very fast,
The tree is covered in cool clear ice,
Like a beautiful young bride surrounded by the choir,
In all their draping white cloaks.

Kayleigh Hardy (14)

MRS WHO?

Disturbed, disturbing lovely lady
                           Heal yourself
Love deprived but love awaiting
                           Love yourself
Crazy mixed up 'kid' that was
                           Don't craze yourself
Beware - the sands of time run out
                           Pace yourself
So many people love you
                           Love yourself

David H Mead

I'll Be There

Look for me when you're lonely;
When the sky is a sorry grey.
When fingers accuse and words bore deep
And the pain won't go away.
Look for me when you're confused;
When the bars grow ever stronger.
When walls close in and dreams are dark,
And the stain of tears gets longer.
Look for me when you need me
And I'll be there for you.
Then when you are gone, I'll think of me
And maybe cry a tear or two.

Michelle Dunnett

TIME/SPACE

The leaves are gone,
We can see the tower
And the time on the clock is clear.
We can tell the hours,
Till the crocus flowers
And hear the song of the stars,
Beyond the reach of the ear
And see the sound of the sea
And touch the taste of fear.

Vera Boyle

CHOOSING YOU
(Written for my dear parents who adopted me when I was ten days old)

When God was choosing me a family,
He took a good look at me,
What I was like in the beginning
And how I'd turn out to be.
A task then set,
Searching the whole world through,
A smile upon his face when he found me you,
Knowing I'd be different, finding it hard to settle in,
The road, quite a rocky one, to travel it I begin.
Two people with commitment and such inner care,
A home so constantly open, such a willingness to share,
A learning process for us all,
Especially for them,
Helping me pick up the pieces after each fall,
Trying not to condemn,
No book of instructions comes with parenthood,
Not even if they're your very own,
You adopted me like no one else ever could,
The non-judgmental caring ways you open up your home,
Where did I go, with whom did I belong,
Why did I mess up, where's my life gone,
But thank you Lord for the family of my own,
For the patience and understanding they've always shown.

Nina Thomas

MOTHER

M others help us look up in life,

O f love, life and kindness.

T hey help us from the first day we are born,
    to the day we're forty.
H er love will make me happy
    and is making me happy.
E very minute of every day she helps us learn
    things in life.
R emembers every little thing from when I first
    walked, to my eleventh birthday.

Vikki Smith (11)

TECHNO PHOBIA

We enter into the 21st century
A nation hell bent on technology
Computers installed everywhere
Microsoft Word, hard and software
All strange words, all strange bits
What are macros and micro-chips?
Surely mackerel swim in the sea
And chips I eat for tea
I wouldn't entertain these in my house
I'd set a trap for that ruddy mouse!
Video recorders, they're as bad
An item I wished I'd never had
Recording a film that's showing late
Ending up with a blank video tape
Then there's CD players with triple trays
What are all these multi-plays?
Just extra buttons to push and press
Causing me even more distress
What's the point of wide screen TV
Half the picture's missing to me
Now the latest invention a DVD
But that's just like another CD
I don't feel well, could it be flu
There's only one thing left to do
Off to bed with cocoa in a mug
Oh no, I've caught that Millennium Bug!

Sally Vale

SILVERDENE COTTAGE

Not imposing, not even quaint,
Far from perfect, with peeling paint,
Brick floors now uncovered, what a sin!
Character abounding within.
Plank doors painted starkly white,
Stripped, gleaming wood overnight.
Cast iron fireplaces boarded away,
Revealed, boldly pretty in light of day.
Spiral stairs begging to be free,
Damp carpet ripped up, bare boards to see.
Tiny back windows open wide
Fresh garden air pervades inside
Empty walls made strong again
To come alive with love, not pain.
Being together, our hopes and dream
In our red brick cottage, our Silverdene.

L Pigrome

PLEASE MAKE IT SOON

When you lose someone it hurts you
You feel sorrow, a physical pain
You realise you can't have them back
And nothing will be the same again.

At first, you can't speak of them
You just think, and then you cry
You wonder how this happened
And then you wonder why

Gradually, the pain eases
You think of them and you smile
You begin to give in to memories
But this takes quite a while

You begin to look at their photographs
And remember when it was taken
You remember times and occasions
And again you feel forsaken

At last, you'll tell stories of them
Your laughter will be a boon
You won't cry when you think of them
Oh God . . . please make it soon.

V J Aldridge

MAITREYA, WORLD TEACHER

Your face, in a magazine,
Unforgettable.
Your message, joy and peace.
Caring and sharing,
The end of poverty and greed.
The realisation
Of the universal dream.

Ursula Johnson

THE SHOE CUPBOARD

Black shiny patent leather,
Brings back the times we danced together,

White satin ones I wore with pride,
The day you took me to be your bride.

The green suede, with heels so high,
To add to my height, I had to try.

The comfy flaties, when we went for a hike,
The bright red ones, you never did like.

Strapy sandals that hurt my feet,
Smart courts to make you look neat.

The boy's football boots, your old slippers,
Even a snorkel, and some flippers.

Each pair has its own tale to tell,
Especially the ones that make your feet swell.

I was going to throw these all away.
Perhaps I'll do it another day.

Myrtle Elden

Research

Offer up a light
undeniable,
keep it in our sight.
Stall the unstable

habits of an age
and communicate
handsomely, the page
has to be paced - wait.

All we need to know
sleeps low, to arise
underneath the flow
of our lidded eyes.

Doug McGhee

THE HALL OF RECORDS

I can not punctuate
so I can not mediate the words between two minds;
I can facilitate a paper place of lines,
I can not modulate these phrases I create
I can not compensate the signs.
I can not calculate
so I can not regulate the visions and the times;
I can but contemplate the station of the rhymes.
I can not arbitrate
so I can not salivate to speak the ties and binds;
I can but cultivate the nature of the crimes.
I can not illustrate
so I can not liberate the pictures in the twines;
I can but terminate the words beneath the spines

Matt Annis

Diss

And does the carillon still play
From the church tower.
Greensleeves on the stroke of nine
Throughout the day on the hour.

Do folk still sit on the seat
Close by St Mary's flint walls.
Their table a tomb as they eat
Food from the old market stalls.

And does the late sun still fall
Over the roofs of town and the mere.
Do swans still glide regally by
Gleaming gold 'neath a lambent sky.

Are candles thick on chestnut trees
Falling softly in the spring breeze.
And do the children still play
In the park at the end of school-day.

Over the sleepy town
Do the bells call the faithful to prayer.
Tell me is it still so, my heart wants to know
For my spirit still lingers there.

With faces and voices of long, long ago
Voices I loved and people I know.
Will this be there in the midst of time
When the exile returns to the old home town.

B Scales

My Granny's Back Garden

'Redbricks' was where my granny lived
A farm cottage, one of three.
The men all worked upon the land
So they lived in the cottages free.
The front gardens were long and full of flowers,
But the back gardens were more fun.
Here potatoes grew and rows of peas,
Their green pods warmed by the sun.
Beetroot and carrots, onions and beans
Sticks of rhubarb, shiny and bright.
Plump, hairy gooseberries, raspberry canes,
Currant bushes, black, red and white.
Apple and pear trees, damson and plum
Tempted my childish hand.
I'd rather be in my granny's back garden
Than *anywhere else in the land.*

Sylvia Southgate

Ever Near

There is no need to stand -
At my grave, stark, and bare,
I am *not* 'asleep' - I am *not* there;

You'll feel me in the winds that blow
You'll see me glinting in the snow . . .
Each tiny jewel, each tiny flake,
Yet - warm as sun - reach every 'ache'.

When first you wake,
Each early morn -
I'm in the new, uplifting dawn;
The chorus of ten thousand birds . . .
These are my voice -
Have not you heard?

Again, return to velvet night,
I am the moon . . . the soft, stars, bright;

So - don't stand by,
Don't shed a tear,
I did not die,
I am not *here!*

Rev Lew Park

UNTITLED

The rain hammers,
smearing the pain.
It reverberates,
again,
inane,
insane,
I drain,
as thoughts of you
return,
I remain,
unmoved
and the sound,
continues.

Amy Phillips

A Period In Time

An aching yearn to have a child,
To give a life through nature's means,
A part of two, resembling both.
A period of time waiting for the day,
A sense of achievement, a sense of bond,
A life-long venture to hang on.

A small cry and sudden shriek, a life's begun,
An individual in their own right.
A few months of sleepless nights.
The sense of joy of those first sights.
Those twos and threes, these years will be!
The joy of response, our teachings heed.

Then comes the tribulations of school,
A loss one can mention with them all,
Independence begins to unravel,
Talents become apparent, parents become distant,
Rival between siblings, teachings become harder.
Nature takes its hold.

Outbreaks a teenager,
No free zone, a muddled time for all,
Each step is an effort, words chosen few.
Sit these years out that's all one can do,
Then comes the break, a child awakes,
Teachings flourish, then all is repeated,
Another cycle begins
The responsibility helps us all,
Through experience each one wins through.

Sheralee Le-Gros

THE ROCK POOL

It's a portrait of the sea
Framed by rocks.
With shimmering, sunlit eyes,
Through fern-green, silken locks.

Pebbles, smoothed and colourful
Are the flesh.
A sea-anemone, the nose,
Soft ripples make a hair-net's mesh.

The ears, two crabs, tucked hidden,
Standing guard.
Courting shrimps move the lips
Once full, through pout, to hard.

Then fingers, poised above
Know it's strange,
But, touch the watery glass
And by doing so, change.

Tricia Cuming

Hunstanton

There's a special calm stillness in the air
The sun is glowing warmth for all to share
Tree branches so still, no breeze to move
All is still, just seagulls flying smooth

Footpaths, roads and promenade all clean and dry
Windscreens sparkle as cars pass by
People walking with a spring in their step
It's days like this we get a lovely sunset

The sea is like a mill pond, almost ripple free
Just waiting for a spectacular sunset to see
The red sun large and round, sinking on the horizon
Lights up sky and sea with colourful glowing beams, all eyes on

The sun colours the water with rays from sun to shore
Sunbeams pierce through the clouds, a beautiful scene to adore
With such brightness of wonderful colours, the sky gleams
Passing through, under and over clouds, how heavenly it seems

Leslie Moate

REFLECTIONS

Sad is the life
that has none to mourn it
when light and life are borne way.
Sad as the leaves fall -
my tears brim and glisten,
grey as the grey day
as life slides away.
Why do I cry and bemoan
your cold death?
Because my dear friend
I had much more to say.

Margaret Adams

Yesteryear - Today - Tomorrow

Born in nineteen hundred and thirty-six,
where in the countryside blackberries were picked
so often by Mum and Dad to boost their income,
to help pay for food when dole was all spent.

Three years old in thirty nine,
as war clouds gathered so quick in time.
To a youngster so little it meant as I recall,
to young men 'twas the time to answer the call.

Men in ships, tanks and aeroplanes, is what we saw
in Pathe pictorial news illustrating this war.
Six years it lasted and so many were lost,
which exposed the acts and what it cost.

When came the end, there were signs of relief,
but for many it left sorrow and grief.
In them who suffered those terrible times;
a deep imprint was left upon their minds.

To assure children that war is not all glory.
Although from it is written many a story,
of heroism, bravery and the ultimate price.
For freedom from tyranny many laid down their life.

When we pause at war memorials, with lists of names
of those who fought and died in war's flames.
A few we may know although many we will not.
Still it remains that they be not ever forgot.

As now in this millennium year,
let all close ranks without fear.
May this Nation of ours be alert and ready,
for the future which will hold surprises many.

Mervyn A Whitmore

MILLENNIUM BUG ALERT!

As the bells ring out, from that famous clock,
Don't let the Millennium Bug, give you a shock,
For don't be fooled, by all the stories you hear,
They were just made up, to cause maximum fear.

Don't go rushing headlong, into panic mode,
While listening to the chaos, out on the road,
Traffic lights going crazy, causing road rage,
Doesn't mean you should worry, just at this stage.

If your domestic supplies, should come to a halt,
Just don't go assuming, that bug is at fault,
A fuse may have blown, for your lights and heater,
Or you might need to pop, ten bob in the meter.

And plunged into darkness, as the temperature drops,
It's time for those candles, you bought at the shops,
Your house now resembles, a giant deep freeze,
And the sound from within, is the knocking of knees.

Now, with careful planning, and thinking ahead,
You won't go hungry, so you needn't dread,
That all your food, will be in short supply,
As you'll have bought enough, to last till July.

And the machine at the bank, will still give you cash,
So your treasured piggy bank, you won't have to smash,
Your computer may crash, with the work you've done,
But it might be a virus, someone put in for fun.

Don't believe the myths, about millennium night,
For the end of the world, is really not in sight,
But a bright new future, will have arrived,
And by January the 2nd, we'll all have survived.

Allison D Fowles

For Keith

I can't believe my fortune, I'm so lucky that we've met,
the perfect night it happened will be one I won't forget.
I suppose the way it came about did not reflect convention,
and falling in love afterwards was hardly the intention.
But somehow it just happened, may it be a twist of fate,
you're the one that I'd been searching for, but you were worth the wait.
As now I can't imagine being with another guy,
we can't be parted in my head, no matter how I try.
I know you don't believe me when I tell you how I feel,
but although I've never loved before, I know when love is real.
You'll just have to appreciate that what I say is true,
and be secure enough to understand that I love you.
I miss you every second of the day that we're apart,
so in these times I keep you locked up safely in my heart.
I consider you my soulmate, my little ray of light,
who's made my life seem happier and made my future bright.
Each moment that I spend with you is pure and utter bliss,
with every feeling, every touch, sealed with a loving kiss.
Our relationship, to me, is something special that's begun,
you're my boyfriend, soulmate, crying shoulder all wrapped up in one.
Just knowing you belong to me, makes me feel such pride,
when I consider the endless qualities you possess inside.
You treat me like a princess and shower me with care,
so now you'll understand why I am sad when you're not there.
I've never felt like this before and in my heart I pray,
that we remain together 'til forever and a day.

Donna

HEAVENLY JUSTICE

I heard a little story once of a lady rich and grim,
who had a humble gardener, and did she humble him . . .

She thought herself above him in her manner autocratic,
till the day they both passed over in her large black automatic.

He had doubled up as chauffeur to save her lots of cash,
but blame was not on him, he did not cause the crash.

When they arrived at heaven's gate, St Peter met them there,
to take them both to their true place, in the next world sphere.

He led the gardener first to a beautiful estate,
which made his former mistress have a heart that did elate.

If that's for him, she thought, what has he got for me?
Who am so much above him, I cannot wait to see . . .

Then St Peter took her to what looked like a shed,
her cry was loud and terrible, and with hands upon her head,

'Do you not know who I am? Please put right your mistake,
however could you bring me here and such a error make?

This is my gardener's place, you have given him my home,
how dare you, dare you, dare you, bring me to this tomb?'

Said Peter 'My dear lady when you on earth do roam,
by love and kindly deeds you build your heavenly home.

The laws of God are truly just, and you must understand,
that all are equal in His sight, all made by His dear hand.

We did our best with what you sent, but kindly deeds were few,
your gardener had a heart of gold, but no kindness from you knew.

He is now reaping his reward for all his Godly living,
if you return to earth again, please learn to be more giving.

Everyone is equal, no matter race or creed,
put yourself in place of others, consider more their need.

Then you will build a heavenly home, one you'll be proud to own,
and will not be ashamed to meet you God upon His throne.'

Madge H Paul

LOVE

Love -
    looked down
        from the cross
    with a yearning
        longing for us -
To love Him too -
        Forever!
  and others as ourselves!

Love -
    looked down
        from the cross
    embracing all the world -
  in His loving, outstretched
        arms!

Christina Miller

TEARS

Tears aren't black and tears aren't white
Tears don't care who is wrong and who's right.
Tears of hunger and tears of pain
But tears won't put things together again.

When will there ever be somewhere that children can all be free?
All we ever see are tiny mouths that are open.
When will there ever be somewhere that children can all be free?
All we ever see are tiny hearts that are broken.

Nowhere to run, nowhere to run to.
Lost their homes, lost their folks, lost their childhood too.
Tears from the child, from a child that is lost in war.
Tears because they don't understand what the fighting's for.

Give them a chance so that they can learn
Give them a chance so that they can turn.
Turn away from the war and walk to the peace
Give them a love, give them a love that will never cease.

Tears aren't black and tears aren't white.
Tears don't care who is wrong and who is right.

David D Bourne

FOR ME

You push aside the darkness
And introduce light
You banish failure
And show me success
You protect me from pain
And give me compassion
You laugh at tedium
And show me magic
You shield me from harm
And protect me
You take away acceptance
And give me pleasure
You make clear confusion
And help me make sense
You break away the ice
And let me feel again
You accept who I am
And like me
You scare away the ghosts
And give me a future
You slaughtered my dark side
And found a princess
I said goodbye to loneliness
And found your love

For you - I smile -
That smile.

Sue Kitson

MOVING AGAIN!

Bungalows, semis, chalets, detached, terrace houses too,
There isn't many left, you have had old and new,
Made new friends, lost the old ones, excitement all the time
Never time to get bored or look back and pine.
Cleaning, gardening, getting straight, the days fly by
What is the sense in it all! I ask you 'Why?'
At least you can look back at all the moves you had
Always something to talk about, really it hasn't been all bad!
Lots of worries and problems, but always a laugh as well
Never know how long you will stay, no one can tell!
A few months, a year, maybe two, time to get the jobs all done
Then it's time to move again and sort out another one,
'Surely,' I say 'this is the last! You won't move again!'
Everything was fine for a while until those neighbours came,
Don't know how you do it, the packing, mess, boxes everywhere,
The years go by, you keep moving, what a wonderful pair.
Mum and Dad, I hope this is the last move, you need a rest,
A bungalow you have bought, I wish you all the best.

Linda Roberts

Untitled

I have lost the thread of the world, let me go back;
Take me by the hand through the dark ages
Up to the dark age, let us stack
The cards up, or do I hold the whole pack?

You must not lose the last trick, I pray;
You must leave me a dark card, and a light;
Otherwise there are no milestones to mark my way,
The night is darkness, and the light is day.

And if the dorsal fin of thoughts and themes
Leads oceanwards to nowhere, turn be back,
And dabble with me in mad mountain streams,
And leave me night, and smother me in dreams.

Mary Colquhoun

THE BOY'S EXAMS

I hate exams
I try my best
But, I never get them right
My teacher says, I should do well
Because, I'm very bright

I hate exams
And even though
I really try my best
I nearly always finish last
Much later than the rest

I hate exams
I try my best
But, why can't teacher see?
I'm better on the football field
That's where I'd rather be!

Tricia Porter

The Grass Is Always Greener

Love we can't have
Feels the strongest,
Hurts the deepest,
Lasts the longest,
Demands the most time,
Develops the fleetest,
Grows the quickest,
Tastes the sweetest.
   The grass is always greener
   On the other person's lawn,
   We all want what we cannot have,
   However high we're born.
Food we can't eat
Tastes the best,
Better farther
Than the rest,
What we see when on a diet
Is appetising to the eyes,
Looks so good, we must just try it,
Every morsel worth a prize:
Every couch potato knows,
When their self-control deserts,
Every ounce of fatness shows,
When food into fat converts.
   The grass is always greener
   On the other person's lawn,
   We all want what we cannot have,
   However high we're born.

Mick Nash

THE SNAIL AND THE FLY

You have heard of 'The Owl And The Pussy Cat;'
but what about 'The Snail And The Fly'?
Fly wished for his own little house
and Snail wanted wings and to fly
he dreamed of flying way up in the sky
past the sun to the moon and the stars
Fly dreamed of 'Home Sweet Home' by the fire -
and a table with flowers in a vase!

In the wood there was a wishing well
they wished hard for their dreams to come true
perhaps 'twas fate that took charge next -
but here is what happened to the two:
An owl swooped down and picked up Snail
and flew high into the sky
while a rabbit digging within the wood
found an old shell which he gave to Fly.

The owl took Snail above the clouds
past the sunset and up-coming moon
while Fly set to work on his new home
and brushed out all the dust with a broom!
When the owl bought Snail back down to Fly
he told of the wonders he'd seen
and Fly showed his house, of which he was proud -
that he'd polished until it did gleam

The moral behind this little tale is:
to never give up on your dreams, some things appear impossible -
but none are as hard as they seem.
Both Snail and Fly lived happy, and told their story to all in the wood.
How do I know? - Well I am that snail
and would do it all again if I could!

Lisa Bristow

GLOBES OF CREATIVITY
(Dedicated to the Shakespeare Globe)

In the distance St Paul's silhouettes against a ray of mystical greys,
a pebbled backdrop mixed with all the passion of the many plays.
Globes of creativity, roofs of Elizabethan beauty, pure and thatched,
to the oak beams, that shelter the talents that will be forever unmatched.

Waters of pride, the caressing bridges of London Tower,
along Pudding Lane, writing words of absolute heartfelt power.
The mist entangles itself in the rain as it beats on the theatre's lights,
it leaves you proud, as it is one of London's most beautiful sights.

The veins of the waves roll gently on low tide,
I look along the waterfront, as tranquillity and peace collide.
Shining like a million sapphires interlaced with a derelict docking bay,
placed against pillars of splendour, that still take your breath away.

The unstirred streets, now chipped by feet of undying haste,
into wayward stations, where life and time has become their waste.
Past destruction, enveloped as the cranes cover the darkened sky,
but not all is lost, as this will be part of our history that will never die.

Daniel North

The Rock

Stood he alone upon the rock
Amidst the ever-rising sea,
The warning wind he heeded not
And he smiled, so sure was he.

This rock so firm beneath his feet
Would place him in no jeopardy,
For this rock was love abiding,
Time and distance was the sea.

From the waters' mass came towering
One great wave, monstrous, deep,
Still he waited, shouting, taunting,
Watched it break against his feet.

Sang he loud in tune with wind song,
Safe am I on true love's land,
But at the dragging of the waters
Oh, the rock had turned to sand.

Down sank he and ever deeper,
In the dark depths drowned was he,
Now the water's smooth and tranquil,
On the sea called perfidy.

P W Pidgeon

The Dream-Land Horse

When night time draws its weary blinds
When starlight and moonbeam begin to shine
A young girl's dreams will start to unfold
Images of fantasy and myths untold
Faraway places will come into view
Blue ribbon rivers, green banks sprinkled with dew

As the girl sleeps she sees in her mind
A shadow by the window
Behind the old hanging vine
Perhaps it is evil or could it be kind
She must go and look while the moonlight it shines
Once out of bed she sees with delight
A dapple grey horse waits for her in the night
His long flowing mane like threads of grey steel
His hot panting breath on her face she does feel
The girl reaches out and touches his brow
The look in his eye tells her come ride on me now
She mounts the horse quickly and to her surprise
He leaps in the air through the night sky he flies
Away to a land where dreams do come true
Past the night time horizon of dark velvet blue

Over star-spangled rainbows that spread down to lost shores
Past crescent moons like beckoning claws
At the back of your mind a new world awaits
Through dreamland's misty garden gate.

Maxine Kaye

JASMINE
(Poem to a granddaughter)

She makes me smile in my hours of darkness
She makes me laugh when I look for hope
She shows me love which helps me hide my sorrows
She is the light that will help me through
When times are bad the thought of her revives my spirit
I will fight on so I can see her growing
She is the one, my own Jasmine
With all her world in front of her, my support
I am sure she will take with her
So Jasmine I will come through these times
That are so hardbearing
With the love you show one day I will give
Back a thousand times
Pray for me as I will pray for you
Laugh with me as I will too
Together we will win
God bless you my own Jasmine

David Phillip Thomas

DEFORESTATION

Inhale I do to take on life's source
This clear, fresh stream taken for granted in our course
Humanity dying out for this unseen
Strength of being from all colours green
Food and water the necessities we see
Why is the world not afraid like me?
We use the natural commodities and rape
The earth's beauty and mysteriousness for our sake
I watch you sway and whisper to me
Is there still time left to save the tree?

Darren Challis

A Walk In The Park

The cherry trees did cover
A rippling, babbling brook
Where we went for walks on Sundays
Across the bridge to a shady nook
And weeping willows tall they stood
So green their branches, protects the wood
Where children play in the park
And we used to sit, till it got dark
So soon the moon and stars were shining
Hardly a sound was to be heard
The birds had gone to nest now
At the end of another day
And the children all gone home
All weary from their play
Then we walked across the bridge once more
And talked about our day
So soon the night is over
Tomorrow is another day

N Carruthers

Hold Your Kitten

Were you holding your kitten tight
As you looked through the window at the moonlight
And were you wishing upon any star
You could change your life for a pop star.

Were you holding your kitten tight
All the way through the eclipse
Simply wishing I wish, I wish
Until the morning came.

Were you holding your kitten tight
So much so that it caught fright
So when it could in the morning it ran away
Now you are lost, well what a day.

Keith L Powell

Friend Or Foe

What's that in the corner
the glass-fronted oblong box
for everyone to stare at
and give it verbal knocks.

It causes many arguments
when we switch it on
encouraging discussions
with ones that we are fond.

Often it's a comfort
when we have nowhere else to go
and sometimes makes us wonder
is it friend or foe.

Some people always have it on
morning, noon and night
many programmes shown to us
give everyone a fright.

Has it maybe indigestion
showing us repeats
is that actress only acting
or been dragged in off the streets.

Could we not write better scripts
or act with more finesse
they are of course paid far too much
I'll send them my address.

It entertains and gives us pleasure
although declare a waste of time
in spite of all I criticise
my TV set's just fine.

Audrey Williams

Autumn Lullaby

Amid the trees an autumn breeze plays a symphony
Everywhere the frosty air is filled with melody
Branches too are swaying like a mighty band
While dancing leaves are spraying golden notes upon the land
Mother Earth so dull and cold watches as they fall from high
Then covered with the leaves of gold she sings an autumn lullaby
The old oak tree with a rumble gently shakes the acorns down
In their thousands they all tumble like fairy pipes upon the ground
Leaves go gaily dancing down shades of yellow, gold and flame
Splashing colour all around like a patchwork counterpane
Twisting, twirling as they fall never-ending from the sky
Mother Earth enfolds them all and sings an autumn lullaby.

Grace Longman

TURMOIL

Trapped, a sweet stolen kiss
feelings abandoned in life's abyss
moorings severed, floating adrift
straining against widening rift
looking hard, searching a clue
mind confused, becoming blue
tough times, fighting the fight
no earthly end in sight
body battered of weary bone
windswept features stand alone
naked emotions face driving rain
lonely soul drenched in pain
desperately seeking to win the war
shackled heart gives no more
hunting a way through the door
solitary beat seeks the core
chink of light, offering hope
feeding dreams, the will to cope
chance to enter, break the seal
fraction of love to hold and feel
burning cold stone of day
once again she turns away
fettered feet climb the slope
hoping for a trace of rope
chasing, fading summer smile
battling on the final mile

Luke Thomas

INVITATION TO LOVE

Awake my love and come with me
Down the lane filled with ecstasy and delight
Where every joy of love can be ours
And where every rapture is in sight.

True feelings can overcome our modesty
When we enter this paradise for two
When we throw our cautions to the wind
In favour of emotions true.

Gerard Oxley

Fire!

Someone left me smouldering
on the sofa, down the stairs.
Soon the lounge will be ablaze
with red, hypnotic flares.

My partner, smoke, has woken,
it's swirling round my head.
It must be time to get to work,
and make these people dead!

The smoke will creep the stairway
and suffocate their dreams
then I will scorch their soft, pink flesh
they won't have time for screams.

Oh no! They must have smelt the smoke
I hear somebody shout.
Now they'll call the firecrew,
to come and put me out.

I hear the wailing sirens
pulling up outside.
They're setting up the hydrant,
there's nowhere I can hide.

The splashing water drowning
and starves the life from me.
Stained black walls and embers
is all that I can be.

Okay! You've beaten me once more,
you think that all is well
you go on living careless lives,
and I'll go back to Hell.

Karen Brooke

Why

We question
The reason why
Our life's partner
Has to die.

We don't get answers
It must be planned
Friends say 'I know
I understand.'

But no, they don't
And they cannot see
It happened, not to them
But just to me.

Until this happens
In your life
Whether loving husband
Or devoted wife.

You don't know
The constant stress
Caused by the
Dreadful loneliness.

B Scotney

HEWN FROM CLOUDS

No hand shall touch that I have made
And fashioned in an enchanted land:
No eye shall see, nor voice shall criticise,
This mystic thing, I have designed and planned.

And none shall know the pleasures and the joys
To be found where only I may go,
No path will e'er be found that leads that way,
For I alone have found and I alone can know.

For I have hewn from clouds to build
And fashioned with a crescent moon my halls
And luminated them with many stars
And tints straight from the rainbow dye my walls.

Daphne Foreman

Red Alert

I open my curtains, a new day is dawning.
The sky is so red, a shepherd's warning.

What are we to do, what will be our fate?
How long has it been, are any actions too late?

No one has prepared me for what is to come.
Will there be damage to livestock, what will be the sum?

Suddenly I remember, for all shepherds I have pity.
But here I am, in a high rise block in the middle of the city.

T A Napper

Fickle

Black Ivan of the fearsome eye,
And jet-black wiry hair,
Admired by all men, young and old,
And loved by passing maidens fair,
Down the road he now is strolling,
With his new love by his side,
See how happily she's laughing,
Pretty cheeks all flushed with pride,
Old loves call him, pleading Ivan
Leave us not, alone like this,
But looking ever on before, stern
He gives them all a miss,
After all he's just a mastiff,
And his beautiful damsel,
Is the new chef at the Queen's Head,
And she feeds black Ivan well.

P Tatley

Dawn

Dawn was breaking with the waves on the feral Murdoch beach,
Sharp November wind blew dark hair o'er ashen cheeks,
She stood cold and naked contemplating the horizon,
Where indefinite clouds bruised the approaching morning sky.

Chilling water lapped over white toes and grey stones,
Deeper. Deeper. The surf breaks across her waist,
The next wave a thousand glassy fingers at her shoulder blades,
And then she is beneath, senses cut by the ancient winter deep.

Blind. Numb. Silent. Bloodless lips whisper bubbles to the abyss,
Motionless now but for the frenzied thump of a dying heart,
Sunrise. Shards of voiceless death all about her, shattering blackness,
Lighting the path to her grave, deep and beautiful.

White waves wash a black soul over grey rocks.
And so time is passing. Days, evenings, nights,
You can stand here as long as you like,
For I doubt you will see her again.

Never forget her though. No, do not forget her when next
The cold, ferocious sea clutches at your ankles
Blind, desperate and wild with primal hunger . . .
For she has not forgotten you.

Matt Deacon

HIDE AND SEEK

When I see you my knees go weak,
I try and hide but your eyes seek.
Your eyes seek but never see,
What these feelings do to me.

I'll play this game of cat and mouse,
My broken heart I'll try and house.
Try and house it because my dear,
It is you that I long to draw near.

Yes, I'll play this game of hide and seek,
I'll play and I'll never once speak.
Never once speak of what is true,
My feelings of love towards you.

Deanna L Dixon

JUST ONE WISH

If I could have one wish: I wish that I
Could write the greatest love song ever heard
A song that sees the nightingale, dear bird
Adopt each note, and to the rhythm fly
A song that tells of love to never die
Of peacefulness and friendships bonded word
So like that dear sweet graceful gifted bird
Mankind would please until the day they die

A song to make the world a better place
A song to nurture care and tenderness
A song that shines new hopefulness and grace
And one that tells of freedom's joyfulness
Sent daily from each beaming upturned face
To thank the Lord for such great happiness.

Violet M Corlett

WRAPPING GRAN

My granny said the other day,
That she wished to go far away,
So when the time came for her to nap,
With paper and string I started to wrap.
I wrapped Gran up from head to toe,
And when she woke she did not know
Where she was or what I'd done,
In fact I'd sent her off to Rome.

Just the next week I received a letter,
My granny said that Rome was much better
Than home at cold and wet Belle Vue,
So why didn't I go and stay there too.
I said that I could not go there,
I'd no more money to pay the fare.
Now I'm dead jealous of my old gran,
She says she's got a smart suntan.

    PS: I wish I hadn't sent her to Rome
           I'd rather have her here at home.

C Lancaster

Vacuum

Out of sight - out of mind
Maybe seem - bit unkind:
Must admit - think it true,
No more see - no think of you.
Something moves - leaves a space,
Something else - takes its place:
Something go - something come,
No more you - vacuum.

Ships that pass - in the night
Only seen by - little light:
In a while - they be gone,
All forgotten - by the dawn.
Waves they roll - to the shore,
Waves big now - soon no more:
Waves they go - more waves come,
No more you - vacuum.

Every cloud - silver lining
'Specially when - sun is shining:
Maybe cloud - break to rain,
Lovely rainbow - come again.
Winds of change - passing by,
Winds that wet - winds that dry:
Winds they go - fresh winds come,
No more you - vacuum.

M R Mackinnon-Pattison

The Elements

The wind thumps against the window
As it roars around the house
The reflection of trees dancing and swaying
As the light from the street lamps
Cast their dark shape on the wall beside me

Doors bang! And the sound of the fan
As the force of the air blows through it
Squeaking and groaning as if in pain
Somewhere a dog barks! A lonely sound
Among the noise of the wind.

Someone shouts and the words
Are torn from their lips
And far away the sound of a train
As it fights its way over Shap Bank
Amid the sound of cars as they swish through the rain

The elements are abroad tonight
Stating their superiority
Wind and rain lashing the countryside
Making us realise yet again
How helpless we are against them

The box in the corner is silent
The arrays of people posturing
And trying to impress with their knowledge
Or lack of it
Silenced! By the elements

I hear again the thunder of the wind
As it rattles the tiles on the roof
As I watch and hear it all
I have the desire to be out there
Among the elements!

Joan May Wills

WHY WEEPEST THOU?

Maiden, why weepest thou? What breaks your little heart?
Has someone told you that your love and you will have to part?
Or has bereavement touched your life with chill and icy hand?
Or someone that you love depart to far and distant land?
Maiden why weepest thou?

The stars all twinkle and the full pale moon shines down,
A sight to gladden any heart,
To bring a smile, not tears or frown,
And yet you weep on still until your throat must ache,
Shoulders hunched and shuddering, a heart about to break,
Maiden why weepest thou?

The moon's reflecting on the sea
As gentle waves caress the shore,
When dawn's soft light comes stealing in
Surely hope returns once more?
As golden wavelets touch the sand,
Soothing as a mother's hand:
You cannot weep forever little maid,
The longest night is always lit by dawn,
Troubles pass and life goes on and on -
Your sister's arm about your neck tries to soothe your fears,
But nothing seems to quench the endless flow of tears,
Oh maid why weepest thou?

You have the precious gift of youth,
And all the beauty of the world is thine,
You think the world has tumbled down about your ears,
You're blind to all the world about or stars that shine,
A prisoner of your sorrow drowning in your tears,
But soon this too shall pass away,
And sorrow be forgotten in the glory of another day,
So maid why weepest thou?

Ailsa Keen

A Patient's Eye View

If you're feeling down,
Do not give up hope.
Leave it to the nurse,
She will help you cope.

Mock not one another,
When they seem distressed.
Depression is an illness,
That cannot be surpressed.

When you're feeling better,
Do not give advice.
Leave it to the experts,
Just try being nice.

Teach yourself to listen
Know when to laugh or weep.
When you share a problem,
Troubles seem less steep.

Jill Ives

Spring In The Air

Just sit down quietly in a meadow and let the world go by,
Feel a gentle breeze upon your face, hear the buzzing of the fly.
Watch cows grazing without speaking just pulling at the grass,
A dog barks in the distance as you let this moment pass.

You can smell freshness in the air and hear lambs bleating,
It's as if you were awakening here and a new world greeting.
Overhead a plane is passing scratching lines in clear blue sky
All of which is possible whilst you let this moment by.

Hear bumblebees, busy, collecting nectar for their hive,
Darting 'twixt the celandines not knowing nine to five.
Birdsong from the missel-thrush turns your thoughts around
As you sit and listen to these very special sounds.

In the trees around this meadow rooks and crows build nests on high,
If they go up any further they will have built them in the sky.
As this springtime's getting started and life's cycle pedals on,
Just sit and ponder where this moment would have gone?

For if you'd missed this meadow whilst rushing past so near,
You would have missed this moment and seeing what was here,
Here, in a world so real which we all tend to ignore,
You must hold onto this moment because it's what life's for.

Now that you've found this secret to the real side of life
Much better armed you'll be to tackle stress and strife.
For when work gets on top of you and you think you'll drown
Go out and find *your* meadow and just *sit down.*

J W Holmes

A Special Thanks To All The Nurses Everywhere! God Bless You

There are some special people whom I have found,
So honest and trustworthy, professionally sound.
No need for names, no personal address,
They are so special - simply the best!
Of all whom I have known
And could selectively prefer
There's only one,
A special one:
It's her!

Her gift is kindness, understanding and care.
Many thoughts, troubles, humorous talk and compassion we share.
She inspires me with confidence in the human race
With a radiant warmth she reflects in 'her' face!
Of all that I have known
To have by my side in times of fear
It is 'her' who is the one, always so near.
There's only one,
A special one:
It's her!

When I have been in need, responded to my call,
Understood my failings, given me 'her' all.
To me she is so precious, her devotion so sincere.
An inspiration to others throughout each changing year.
An angel to all who may need loving care.
The comfort in knowing that 'she' is always there,
Of all the best that I have known
On whom my life I did confer
There's only one,
A very special one:
It's her!

Tony W Rylatt

THROUGH THE AGES

The school concert theme in December nineteen ninety-nine
Was an excellent review of all the millennium outline
'Through The Ages' portraying scenes from Anno Domini
When the baby Jesus was born which no one can deny
The story over the years is still practised with good will
Praising and thanking God all over the world at Christmas time
                                                                                         so tranquil
Then moving on from the bible stories to the scene of explorers
                          and discoveries also characters of the past
Like Christopher Columbus who sailed the high seas and found
                                          a continent so vast
To Shakespeare, Picasso and the Mona Liza in the world of art
The musical entertainment and sport in the nineteen sixties was all part
Of the World Cup football match plus pop groups and stars
Not forgetting Elvis with his rock and roll guitar.
Moving on into the twenty-first century and finally orbited into space
When our memorabilia journey 'Through The Ages' ended walking
                                               on the moon's face.
All cleverly produced and acted to music with costumes to tone
An excellent performance and perhaps in the future a trip to
                                             the unknown.

Nancy Owen

THINKING OF CLOUDS

Can it be that those rolling clouds
Hold, as the salt, so much moisture?
When, windblown, they break upon a bank, a hill
And lose their contents on the world.
How odd that those so frail
Are as one with the powerful salt
For that too, when windblown
Breaks upon a bank, a cliff
And sprays the earth.
So each carries the evolving instrument
Of water and so life proceeds
Wet!

John Aldred

AN ISLAND OF DREAMS

Memories from the past
Children's laughter
Running through the sand
Finding treasured shells
A tortoiseshell shines in the sun

Watching the waves gently roll
leaving glistening stones
Precious gems of the sea
Sea horses galloping through the mists of time
Starfish forming patterns
A circle of pearls.

Betsey Prose

JACK FROST

Ice-cold, snowy fingers,
Winter lingers
On. Jack Frost waves his wand
Ice grows on the pond.

Icy patterns, scritch and scratch,
No other artist can match
Jack working on his masterpiece
All night long - he does not cease.

Spiky tendrils, little swords
Piercing hoar -
Frost and freezing lances,
Round and round that Jack Frost prances.

Dancing, leaping, jumping, creeping
Ice is seeping
Into every crevice, nook and crack:
None escape the mighty Jack!

Icy fingers, never heard,
Drawing pictures, writing words,
All mysterious, but say the same:
Jack is out and it's his game.

Dawn arrives and Jack moves on
To pastures new to draw upon.
Setting sun and cooling day,
Jack returns, his games to play.

Kathryn J Hayward

SMOKE CONTROL ORDER
(A resident's lament)

O-yez! O-yez! O-yez!
Hear-ye! . . . Hear ye! . . . Loyal people of this village hear-ye!
By official decree of the 'powers that be'?
We have got to go smokeless!

Our chimneys offend, with smoke that ascends
In the air they say is polluted.
Let's tarry awhile; when we 'put on the style'
I wonder will all be suited?

No smuts here and there to sully the air,
I've no doubt they think that's terrific.
We still will be fed our quota of lead
From exhausts of vehicular traffic.

A sad farewell.

To the bright dancing flames,
(Remember . . . ? We played those fire picture games)
And the cosy glow when the coals burn low
And the warmth of the room next morning.

'Now what do we do with the shovel and rake?'
When under this law we knuckle,
The brush and the tongs? Paper and wood
And the pride of the hearth . . . the coal scuttle!
The coal that's left over when that fatal day dawns
And we are no longer the 'stokers', well! nobody cares
So we're stuck with our wares.
'Oh! What can we do with the pokers?'

But, alack and alas we have to heed 'em,
While they chip a bit more off our freedom.
On that cold November dawn, I for one will sadly mourn.

The passing of old king coal.

Florence Taylor

EERIE

Heart beating ravenously;
A grisly restlessness,
I'm stuck with it
Through sickness and sin,
I know I won't win.

There's a voodoo in the night,
A horror if it had sight;
I know I'm right,
I've learnt from the light.

Something treads through the gardens
At the day's back,
I'm waiting for an attack;
My imagination has no lack
Of competence.

A lost angel
At a human angle?
Terror jangles;
My nerves form me.

Charles Butler

THREE LIVES

the train stops suddenly
a woman, holding a baby
waves from across the lane
a white horse moves uneasily in a field
smoke escapes from a large stone house
ahead, where the track turns
a neglected church

all off, everybody off, please . . .

no signposts
under a tired Judas tree, abandoned
almost flush with the ground
at the mercy of wind and rain
three graves

three mysteries
pilgrims perhaps, returning from the Holy Land
struck down by Black Death

the stone carvings are unusual
one, a latticed pattern
under a figure with crossed arms
the other, a rope
running the length of the coffin stone
the third, a man in a short tunic
barefoot, a sword in his belt

here, at the end of the lane, history stalks
no traffic noise
only the cry of a curlew in the marches below
bleak, as the gales come in from the estuary

now
back on the train
three lives haunt my imagination.

Alfa

LATE AUTUMN

The autumn leaves lying dead on the ground
Crackle as my footsteps pass over the mounds.
The colours of the fall have faded away,
And withered foliage blows astray.

The sound and the feel of the crunch underfoot,
Takes me back across the miles of years,
To leafy lanes and suburban pathways
I trod with my boots and gaitered legs.

The branches bare, stretch black fingers to the sky,
From long crooked arms and knotted tree trunks.
There's a harsh chattering cry, of a crow or magpie,
As he flies to and from his nest up on high.

The snap of a twig as I walk in the woods,
On a thick bed of leaves on the earth, breaks the silence.
Odd chestnuts and walnuts still lie on the ground
And will soon rot away for manure,
To feed the majestic, glorious trees,
Who'll delight us once more in the spring,

But now I stroll in my muffler and gloves
Wrapped warm for winter is nigh,
And breathe in the beauty of crisp late autumn,
With the sun low down in the sky.

Josephine Moreau

A Time To Run

In days of old when knights were bold
Television was just a child
Those were the days it was safe to play
Quite often we ran wild
With bat and ball and wheel and sticks
A matinee we watched, Tom Micks
It was a happy time, the war was done
A minor miracle we had won
My shoes and clothes were hand-me-downs
A big red nose and I'm a clown
My friends and I, we roamed the street
As cobbled stones lay beneath my feet
We had no marvels of a time to come
We were children at play, we loved to run
Not for us computer games
No hyper space to rot our brains
It was a simple time with simple ways
On the street was where we spent our days
Now here I sit, keyboard at hand
Thought and deed at my command
I remember the time I used to run
That was a different time . . . a different sun.

Roy McCadden

THE SADISTS

Those sadistic fiends on horseback,
Who believe in 'repent ye not';
Who get their kicks from the sight of blood,
No matter how it's begot!
Who delight in inflicting pain,
As long as it's not theirs;
But of some unfortunate fox,
That's been caught unawares!
Urged on by the devil's horn,
O'er hedge, through field and beyond;
With the frenzied pack almost dripping blood,
In the chase for the fox, long gone!
To close, and kill, in the name of a sport
Created by the devil;
With a fervour, such, that evil reigns,
For to 'befriend' is above their level!
Yes, if only 'they' for once could be
Their quarry for the day;
To be torn to pieces just for fun,
Would 'damnation' win the day?
But whether or not, in life,
Retribution will come to those;
Only time alone will tell,
For only 'heaven' really knows!

B Colebourn

LOVE

Most precious things in life are free,
So keep loving, that's the key.
Look forward to the future,
Enjoy the present day.
For tomorrow never comes,
Nor does yesterday.
Let all the world rejoice,
All in one big voice.
To wish you all the best in life,
With happy times and little strife.
True love will never die,
Although the years will simply fly.
Enjoy your magic times together,
And may it last you all forever.

Geraldine Ward

ANTE MILLENNIUM

When Christ was born they called it year one
And from that time onward the counting was done.
History was made as the years rolled on
First Celts, then Romans and Anglo-Saxon
Followed by Danes and Vikings who were overcome
When Harold the battle of Stamford Bridge won.
In turn he was killed in 1066 by William the Norm.
While Richard I on crusade had gone
The Barons revolted and his brother John
Had to sign Magna Carta, in 1215 this was done.
There were two more Richards, Yorkshire's own
Before Lancaster's Henry wrested their crown.
Of the Tudors Henry VIII was best known
For having six wives, two daughters, one son
Who died as a boy; Queen Bess reigned alone
In 1588 she sent the Armada to a watery home.
Having no heirs the Stuarts came to the throne.
Charles I lost his head, Cromwell's Commonwealth began
The civil war. The Roundheads the country overran.
But the Stuarts returned, Charles II, James II and Anne
Then William and Mary; followed by Hanoverian
George I, II, III, the last was mainly known
For losing America and to madness was prone.
The Empress Queen Victoria for sixty years wore the crown
Her daughters married foreign kings, Edward VII was her son.
Grandchildren were English George, Kaiser Bill and
                                      Nicholas the Russian
In 1914 they fought each other, for four years war went on
Lessons were not learnt, in 1939 another war was begun
In 1953 Elizabeth II came to the throne
And has reigned in peace from that day on.

Lisa Wolfe

No More Mr Nice Guy

No more Mr Nice Guy
In a world that doesn't care
No more Mr Nice Guy
In a world no longer there

In a world where Mr Nice Guy
Is treated like a fool
And Mr Nasty feted
For actions base and cruel

Where kind is soft
And nice is weak
And being a gent
Is thought a freak

Where drugs are cool
And vice inviting
Where sex is king
And crime exciting

No more Mr Nice Guy
No more Mr There
No more Mr Nice Guy
No, someone has to care.

Tony Sheldon

Perseverance

Life is like a battle with victories to be won
Arm yourself with fortitude until the job is done
Make no friend of failure it leaves you feeling poor
Always aim to have success it opens every door

Never give up trying always struggle on
Remembering that if you don't
Your chances may have gone
Never be defeated try your best to win
Give it everything you've got
Never just give in

Barbara Hampson

Nouveau Riche (Noo-Voh Reesh)
Queen: Know What I Mean?

I know you believe I spend like there's no tomorrow
But don't you want me to be happy with no sad sorrow?
It's not as if I go all out on a spending spree
You've money in the bank and I just want to make you happy.

I've seen the latest style in the centre of fashion
And it's not as if there's any need for you to ration
I want to wear what shows me off best just for you
You know you can be nice if you really love me true.

Just give me a sign that things will soon change
Though we live together we're going out of range
Sometimes I play at being your sweet honey flower
While time is running out towards the eleventh hour.

What wouldn't I do for a few nights on the town too
I want to let my hair down for all to view
Now I'm a part of the trendy nouveau riche (noo-voh reesh)
I want to give it a good go and create my own niche.

I want to flirt and I want to make them all stare
To meet others who too have feelings to share
I've tried so hard to make him understand just how I feel
Yet he gives me an old fashioned look and just turns his heel.

My mind turns to the time when the sun never set on our scene
And the sun shone forever on our warm love passionate yet serene
How I long for the time when nothing ever came to spoil our love
So near yet so far as I try to recapture the flight of the dove.

I'm just a nouveau riche (noo-voh reesh) girl why can't you see?
I love spending for fun it sends me into such sweet ecstasy
I love to move and groove and let the best parts of me show
Before time changes the real image of the inner me you know
I know if you try you will see what I really mean
Or have we both lost the last chance of sharing our own scene?

Jackie Docherty

DESTINY

I am the lyric writer
  music rules my soul,
I smile writing the lyrics
  shed tears when the moon is whole.

Immortal words spoken
  in a shallow world
Watching the emptiness
  feeling the silence
Shedding the tears
  yet feeling the warmth
Knowing the sadness
  yet feeling love
Hearing the lies
  yet knowing truth
Walking dark pathways
  yet seeing the light
Generating a mystique
  is being unique
Knowing there is a devil
  in believing in God
Seeing hate in the world
  yet generating beauty

Love of a past and future age
  see and know I care
For as I now create that beauty
  in that truth I am living there.

J W Anderton

CAME THE RAIN

When young days
Were about us
With laughter
On sweet
Scented breath,
And the moon
In your hair
In your eyes,
You were the moon.
But came the rain,
And afterwards
Half forgotten
Laughter
Drifted upon me
With
Your memory.

R Smith

ISOLATION?

Years ago we used to meet
Shoppers in our village street.
Mouth-watering smells of baking bread
The best in Lancashire, it's said,
Lured us to the little shop
Where gossip thrived and kindly chat
Passed the time for lonely folk
Enjoying company. All that
Has gone. We stay inside our house
And order groceries, with a mouse.

Muriel Berry

LISTEN TO ME

When I have gone away
where you can never find me -
when you will not meet me
walking through the park
or in any street -
when I no longer smile at you
coming down the path -
go to the rowan tree in the garden
and listen for me there.

I will speak to you
with the blackbird's voice
as my father still speaks to me.
When I walked with him in the wood
I heard that lilting music
like the juice of a ripe blackberry,
he taught me to listen for it -
to know it from other songs.

We were in no country place -
oak leaves were blackened by the pit
but the voice of the blackbird
came to my ears as pure as mountain water -
a natural sound like a father calling to his child.

Deirdre Armes Smith

SEVEN

What is so special about the number seven?
We talk of being in seventh heaven;
Our lives are made up of seven ages of man;
God rested on the seventh day. That's how it began.

God made the world. It has seven wonders,
Upon which one looks with awe and ponders
On their grandeur, their magnificence.
Why does seven have such significance?

Long ago brave men crossed the seven seas
In their sailing ships, praying for a stiff breeze
To carry them to the seven continents of the world,
Where they staked their claims with banners unfurled.

The colours in the rainbow number seven,
Such a glorious sight, a sight from heaven
Which God gave to Noah to show the flood was o'er;
He and his kin could resume their lives once more.

Extraordinary powers which may have us beguiled
Has the seventh child of a seventh child.
And so it goes on. Is it just coincidence
That we have all these 'seven' incidents?

Marlene Allen

THE FOG

Sometimes I hate it,
I can't find the way,
To create the thing,
That will make me stay.

I don't know what it is
Or where it's hiding,
One thing I know,
I believe it's frightened.

We expect so much,
Our hopes are high,
We get so little,
The fog never dies.

Susan Jenkinson

GETTY'SBURGH

Dusted o'er akin to phantoms there afoot,
All sure advancing to the stirring rhythm
Of the drums that led the weary men
And sided there to 'Yankee' flags
Of regiment, company and troop, unfurled.
Steadfast strode the blue-clad youth,
Unto the eager-waiting guns and truth.

Yonder 'rise' so very soon to vent upon unyielding flesh
Such hell of shot and seeking, searing ball
Sent swift and sure upon its deadly way.
There upon the bloodied soil
Wouldst brave men cease all earthly toil.

Honour bestowed unto the guiding, throbbing beat
And burnished steel affixed - prepared this hour
To cruel enjoin within the battle's heat.
Come - they now those young men garbed in dusted blue,
Confrontation dire with others clad in greyish hue,
But hearts with valour-bent ne'er didst pause
As redden'd blades avowed each other's cause.

Stumbling oft' but rising swift once more
And then to stride again 'til fatal touch lays low
'Pon field of death 'midst screaming, cursing men
Who knew the kiss of 'reaper's' callous blade.
This day wouldst be the final one,
No more for them the rising sun.

History wouldst recall such day . . . of those
Who went upon such sadly way towards the battle's din
And knowing not their coming fate.
'Tis certain they'd not care for such decree
That someday hence wouldst tell their tale to you and me.

Dennis F Tye

SPRING

Nothing is so beautiful as spring
The springtime air feels fresh and warm
And the rainclouds sometimes fall in soft gentle showers
The secret consolation is the image of descending earth's sweet being.

There are so many daffodils in garden array
With the colour of the sun they help to brighten the day
They surely make us see that spring is really here,
The earth smells sweet with the scent of flowers.

Sitting in the brightness and scowling in the glare
The glassy pear tree blooms in the air
The descending blue charm, it can soothe the cheerfulness of delight
Could not but compose the image of the multitude secret.

Heather Aspinall

To A Swift

O! Swift dark denizen of summer sky
Unlike the swallow with its flash of white and blue,
Larger and of more sombre hue
Forever wheeling o'er where waters lie.
Oh! Restless soul that's ne'er a moment still
When rest you or seek a lull
From turning, twisting aerobatic skill?
They say you even sleep on wing and ne'er alight.
We know the insect cloud is subject of your frenzied flight
And perhaps when satiety comes you cease your restless quest,
But to the unsuspecting eye
'Tis all as pointless as an unborn cry.
Just like my heart forever on the move
It knows no meaning nor no goal,
No feast comes into view nor balm to soothe
Is there no rest, no home, no solace for my soul?

Eddie Sykes

THE LOVE WITHIN

If you open the door to your heart
You will see a wondrous scene,
And if you open it wide enough,
You will be sure to find your dream.

Make it easy for loved ones to enter,
Leave the door ajar.
Release all the love you have in you
So that it may travel afar.

Jack Ryan

TOBY
(The 'Noble Man' of Cumbria!)

You are so kind and loyal and would never judge.
In the old days from the field you would not budge.
You weren't being wicked, just more interested in eating.
Though you enjoyed work, the taste of grass took some beating.

Now you meet us with that quizzical look as if to say
'I'll come on in today, for I know I won't get my own way.'
You're always happy to see us 'cos we've carrots and polos to eat.
You know very well that only well behaved horses are given such treats.
You've never been bad, just full of youthful beans
And it's obvious to us all that jumping is in your genes.

You stand there so patiently while being groomed and saddled up
And don't even complain when your girth is tightened up.
You are always raring to go - either in the school or out for a hack.
Knowing you'll come to no harm with Emma on your back.

While out in the lanes you look at everything in sight.
Peering over hedges is simple with your great height.
It's all so new and exciting wondering what's round the next bend.
Fiddling all the time with your bit as on your way you wend.

You love being included in all our conversations
And if we dare to ignore you, you soon lose your patience.
You've got such a big heart and wouldn't hurt a fly
But if we don't talk to you, you feel left out and want to know why.
You listen to everything that is being said
Flicking your ears back and forth on your handsome head.

You know you've got it made when you get back in the yard
For there are more polos and carrots - oh, life is so hard!
Then it's in your stable to see what you can find.
Hay and a bucket of feed - what a wonderful way to unwind!

As you stand there slowly munching away
You see other horses in the field and give them a neigh
Saying life is so good when you are so handsome
And how glad you are that your name is Toby Thompson.

You're the best horse in the land - you know you are
And if you keep up the good work, I know you'll go far.

Judy Buxton

WHY ME

I see from afar all standing there
What in common do they share
I see my wife and children and friends
All gather round as I descend

With heads bowed all dressed in black
They huddle together back to back
For whom do they surround the grave
Mastering their sorrow so very brave

I felt their sorrow, their hurt and pain
Searching for someone they look in vain
A loved one's departing it is clear
Family and friends are grieving here

I feel a sudden surge of dread
A thought, a fear inside my head
And flashing there before my eyes
See my wife, I hear her sighs

Why am I not within the crowd
I hear a father pray out loud
As the coffin's lowered in departure
Farewell words requiescat in pace

I look upon the coffin lid
At the inscription previously hid
The name plate etched into it
My dear late husband John James Prewett

Jim Preston

A Pleasing Power

My mind ever yearned to see what others see,
A pleasant wander in woods and farms, to seek,
The sight of nature's plans, of spring dominate,
Quiet fishing, to bond, with the balanced wild,
My seat on two wheels, thirsts for the new,
Each bend, offers unseen view,
Other ages passing through,
Family bred, has want of bread,
Factory life, and all are fed,
Forms and faces, once so dear,
Drift beyond, a silent tear,
Going to where no one knows,
Time's highway, ever flows,
Not too fast and not too slow,
Time's alive, who made it so,
Four score signpost, is no more,
Nature's show, not seen before,
Distant scene, comes in view,
A warmer air, kerbs winter's chill.
Soft clouds weep, my daffs a-peep,
A flowing energy, for life,
Warm wet sun, sees winter done,
Wood knows, to power the cells,
Power, effervescent, saturating, live.
An energy, exploding, silently,
Spring, satisfies all, a delight,
Winter, will turn off the power,
Time is wringing my bell, I fear
Life, grows, 'tis alive, an everlasting force,
Each day a new bloom, so very new.
So peaceful my garden.
'Tis good for me and you.

H Cotterill

PMS

It's not just pain and periods,
but mental strain as well.
You can't explain to anyone
cos it's very hard to tell.

I wake up with no feelings
just a low depressive state.
Where I yell and scream at everyone
it's this part I really *hate*.

I know I'm being moody
and a bitch is what I am.
I try my very best,
well the very best I can.

I tell myself to cheer up,
stop being such a bore.
But the harder that I try this
it just makes me worse some more.

The things we do in daily life,
they always seem so grim.
It's like someone's taken my emotions,
they've gone, from deep within.

It's hard for me to laugh and smile,
like I always used to do.
I want it to be spontaneous
not just doing it to cue.

Some days I just hate everyone,
it's an awful thing to say.
I feel like packing up my bags
and going on my way.

I feel all alone,
with this other side of me.
Oh! I wish I could feel better,
like the way I used to be.

My family! You know I love you,
I love you more than words can say.
And I hope you can forgive me
when I act in this weird way.

Mandy Parker

SWINTON FIELDS

We called them Swinton Fields,
Swinton people called them Eccles,
the official name was Ellesmere Park.
In the evenings or weekends
you left the tall Victorian houses,
past the white gates,
into green fields, the ponds,
the hoardings round the Rugby ground.
Strolled over to Black Harry,
the smoke-grimed tunnel,
under the disused rail-track
where couples lingered.
From the higher ground beyond
you saw, surrounding on all sides
the factories, mills, the smoking chimneys,
the essence of our working life.

R E Fairclough

SEARCHING

I search for the face
That I long to see,
The one in the world
That matters to me.

So long since I saw you,
Yet you're always with me,
The face in a million
That forever haunts me.

Are you there in the crowd
That is all around me?
And are you searching too
For the face that is me?

If you should just turn
And catch sight of me,
Would mine be the face
That you long to see?

Joyce Brown

COME MY LOVE

Come with me
O come my love,
The moon is shining
High above,
The velvet night
Holds out her arms,
Inviting us
To share her charms,
The nightingale so sweetly sings
Of magic spells
And fairy rings,
The stars come out
To light our way
To the mossy couch
Where we shall lay,
We two will be
Entwined as one,
Body, heart and mind
until awakened by the sun.

Carole H Sexton

MYSTERY OF SPACE

Mystery all around when rocket ships
Leave the ground

A rocket ship flies up in space
On and on to win the race,

Round the world ever so high
Far out in space men could die,

Space stations among the stars
Even planets one called 'Mars'

Flames aglow from their tails do burn
From outerspace science inventors look and learn,

Through telescopes and glasses to school boys
Dreams could come true,

To find one day among the stars
Another planet just like 'Mars'

To name just one of many so high up in space
In the galaxy of stars,

Moonbeams and sunbeams travel so fast speeds of light
Ever so near

Now that the data is so clear.

Elizabeth A Wilkinson

DISTRESS! (OR, THE LIFEBOAT)

The screeching, tearing wind reached out angrily
And in its jaws caught the heaving foamy sea.
The little boat had lost the will to live
And the captain hadn't any more to give.

Madly roared and tumbled the soaring brine,
Then suddenly out of Hell was thrown a line:
Grim-faced men with all their combined strength and might
Were urging him frantically to hold on tight.

The lifeboat had braved the stormy, stormy seas,
Sight of which, the captain fell upon his knees,
But the sturdy coxswain of the lifeboat knew
They still had a mountain of work to do.

The wind tore and shrieked like a great frenzied beast.
To the weary crewmen that wasn't the least.
The lifeboat went into a gargantuan trough:
How in the world were they to get him off?

Then a crewman in an oilskin, yellow,
Volunteered himself - the plucky fellow,
A family man - to slide down the outstretched rope
Into the captain's quickly sinking boat.

Whipping the darkness, the wind shrieked and howled
And to all the crewmen, grim and grey jowelled,
The nightmare of the heaving night had begun,
To try and save this most unlucky human.

Inch by inch the crewman edged along the rope;
All the rest could do was only pray and hope.
With each breath taken and knocked out of his body
He wished himself in bed with a hot toddy.

Every tortured moment was felt in pain,
And the men prayed it wouldn't be in vain,
Because the captain's boat was sinking fast.
Ah! They saw he'd managed to reach her, at last!

The captain helped the man as much as he could:
He wasn't much use - his frozen hands felt like wood.
But, when the ordeal was past, on the lifeboat
They gave him a stiff drink and a big warm coat.

Tossing, twisting and turning, in the fierce gale
The bobbing lifeboat seeming so small and frail
Heading back for home and a bright friendly fire,
Until next time someone needed its help, dire!

J Millington

Butterfly Heart

A cold shell
Hid so well the butterfly heart
That fluttered
Fragile wings, which tore
A little more with each sharp word
He uttered.
Etched lines
The tell-tale signs of bitterness
On her face
Hard and white,
Arms folded tight and which never gave
A child embrace.
Older now,
I understand how we all need to feel a
Tender touch
To pass on to another
And that deep within, my darling mother
You really loved me very much.

Jane Solan-Robertson

FEATHERED FRIENDS?

Swooping down
Like some feathered army,
The troops arrive for food.
Greenfinches
Skirmish among themselves
For their supply of seeds.
Blackbirds pounce,
Looting bread and apple,
Repel rival starlings.
Blue tits cling.
The peanut holder sways,
Commandos raid for nuts.
A red flash.
The robin scouts around
Behind enemy lines.
Undaunted,
Sparrows advance to find
There's not much booty left.
Shadows fall.
The sparrowhawks muster,
Seeking out tiny prey.
Scattering,
Feathered army retreats
To fight another day.

Angela Pritchard

My Little House

Oh little house I thank you
   for your shelter through the years
For the warmth and comfort you've given us
   through our laughter and our tears
For being there when I needed you
   and for giving me a new start
Oh little house I thank you
   from the bottom of my heart.

Oh little house I thank you
   for the opportunity
To bring stability into the lives
   of the ones most dear to me
For the walls that kept us safe within
   for the windows and the door
For the hearth that gave a cheery glow
   till the storm had passed once more.

Oh little house I thank you
   for the happy atmosphere
That still pervades throughout the rooms
   keeping loved ones ever near
For the sense of security you've given us
   and for seeing us safely through
For all these things oh little house
   I sincerely truly thank you.

P Tattersall

Lost Child

What has happened to the little girl that I once knew
Where did she go?
Was it so long ago when she was my own sweet child?

Now she stands before me, this child-like woman
This stranger to my eyes
Full of rebellion, resentment
Honesty now lost in too many deceitful see through lies

Her room has become sanctuary
Where she shuts herself away
Do not disturb, do not enter, keep out
Now mean just exactly what they say

I live in hope that our daughter
Will realise how alienated she has become
And return as part of our family
Excepting that we are not the enemy
But simply Dad and Mum.

Patricia Brown

Changing Seasons

Snow on the hilltops, frost in the dales
Closely followed by rain and the gales,
Winter is changing into spring,
Flowers peep through and birds do sing
Sunshine peeping over the cloud,
Gardeners digging with their heads bowed
Weather unceasing, continually changing
Plants and weeds need re-arranging
Last year's dead-heading that didn't get done
These endless jobs go on and on
Weeds will need pulling and the lawns mown
When seeds are planted and newly sown
Sit down and relax, look at the border
Everything complete and now in order

Marion Pollitt

THE SEASONS

Happy April days
Enjoy each fleeting hour
Savour the blossom decorating the trees
That fragrant first spring flower

Soon the season will change
Summer will be here
Beautiful still but more mature
The middle of the year

Roses will be blooming
They always do in June
Bringing that touch of perfection
The fear they will fade too soon

There will still be weeks of summer
Before the autumn is nigh
When the shades of the leaves will be golden
As they fall to the ground with a sigh

Cold dark winter will slowly creep in
When our beautiful world seems to die
To arise in the glory of spring again
Winter to defy.

Bunty Yates Aldred

WHO AM I?

I'm a human, terran, earthling too
My name could be Holly, Amy, Paula or Sue.
My species come in so many varieties
All of us belong to different societies
Our eyes could be black, brown, green or blue
We each prefer a different shoe.
We pride ourselves with our individuality
But some should wake up, and face reality.
All of us should be taught at school
That war is violent, harsh and cruel.
Life is precious, and not to be wasted,
So why are animals cubed or pasted?
The answer to this, I don't think you will know,
Our species have evolved and continue to grow.
I wonder if by the year 3001,
The earth will be wiped out, completely gone.
By then we could have travelled to the stars,
And left behind what is rightfully ours.
So when an alien asks who I am,
I could be Rachel, Sarah, Melissa or Sam.
We should keep a good standard of morality
And always hold on to that individuality.

Holly Stewart (13)

A Prayer For The New Millennium

At the start of a brand-new year -
Dear Lord, we pray . . .
For unity amongst Christians everywhere,
For a deeper love for one another,
Help us to speak the Gospel without fear,
Help us to live lives worthy of Your calling,
We ask You to revive Your church -
Shake us, stir us, mould us, Lord -
Make us the people you want us to be,
Help us to live by the power of Your Spirit,
Draw us closer to You,
Help us to be dependent on You -
For we can't achieve anything in our own strength,
Show us how to put Your love into action,
Help us to be doers of Your Word -
And not just hearers of Your Word,
Help us to fix our eyes on the unseen,
For that which is unseen is eternal,
When life seems difficult and hard -
Cause us to remember that . . .
You will never leave us or forsake us,
Strengthen our faith, Lord,
Help us to put our complete trust in You,
For You are the Alpha and the Omega -
The first and the last -
The beginning and the end.
Amen

Yolande Hall

Nu-Speak

Why be coy about your age?
It's more than just a date,
The words you use, the terms you choose,
Will set the record straight.

You may thing life's been good to you,
Your mirror says, 'You're great!'
But, if you need to move from home,
You have to 'relocate'.

In times gone by, a 'town house'
Was a 'terrace' in a row,
Flats now are 'dwelling units',
Up and down in lifts we go.

To make a contact swiftly
Use the 'internet', how classy!
'Visit the website' with 'fax' and 'e's'
To telephone is passé!

Look into any pram these days,
With a 'coo', and a smile that's merry,
You won't find an Arthur, or a Gladys there,
But a 'Sharon', 'Wayne' or a 'Kerry'.

So, be brave and true and forthright,
Don't be slow to state your years,
So much can give the game away,
Much more than first appears!

So, 'give your best shot' 'at the end of the day',
'At this moment in time' contemplate,
In the next fifty years, this 'scenario',
Will be long past it's 'sell-by-date'.

Elizabeth Rapley

NEIGHBOURS 'R' HELL

'Neighbours, everybody needs good neighbours' is how the song goes
But for a vast majority of decent people their lives are full of woes
Let's take a look at my street but it could be anywhere
A slipping, crumbling social breakdown leading to despair
Big Denzil at number ten likes to hold these all night parties
Where dealers hand out drugs like they're only kids' Smarties
Now Ron and Doreen at number twelve argue all day and night
And poor John the punch-drunk fighter is reliving an old fight
Colin in his ice-cream van with that very irritating jingle
Is going to see his floozy who has told the DSS she's single
Old Nellie across the road has turned her home into a zoo
And we call her grandson Bostick because he's always sniffing glue
Every front garden for miles around has its very own scrap car
And it's not much fun believe me shopping at my local fortress Spar
Broken bits of glass bottles, twinkle in the sun and look so pretty
These are what are known locally as the 'diamonds of inner cities'
Graffiti on a house door spells out that we have a pervert living here
But he doesn't anymore 'cause a couple of locals made him disappear
There's a pack of dogs, semi wild, roaming the kids' playground
And Danny Wood who mugged old Jenny, for a lousy stinking pound
Children as young as five are torching anything that will burn
It's really not the sort of thing these toddlers should have to learn
A fly-tipped mattress soiled and stained God knows where it's been
Is becoming a major attraction as the neighbourhood trampoline
A hundred radios all at full blast from Abba to Frank Zappa
Are competing in a decibel war with Mr B the New York rapper
What sounds like rapid gunfire suddenly crackles across the sky
I close my eyes and hope and pray that it's not my time to die
Believe it or not this is England on an estate not that far away
So count your blessings daily and hope my world don't come your way

Michael Bellerby

SMALL AGAIN

Won't be so small again,
Won't be so vulnerable again,
Won't be so defenceless again
And so willing to believe
You want me . . . again.

Coming to angry words again,
Coming to the point of nothing
And the frustrated silence
Of pregnant violence
In a look again.

Won't be glad to give again,
Won't be lacerated and bled dry
And still asking,
'What more, if not I?'
Won't be capable of loving again.

Paula Morris

THE BEAUTY OF THE MORNING

As light comes bursting through the clouds
branches spread out from the trees, and heads peep
from the petals of the flowers in all their jest
and birds in their nests begin to sing.
But 'tis not perfect morning lest:
The azure of the sky to the morning doth bring
as it floats gently to the sea.

The gentle breeze which sweeps your hair
the dewdrops upon every blade of grass,
the perfect fragrance of cool clean air
and the patter of little creatures which swiftly pass.
The sun which warms these gifts adorning
decks the beauty of the morning.

Julie Gaskell

EARLY SPRING

Spring has arrived early this year,
Promising fresh delightful cheer.
Snowdrops bending their heads in bloom,
Colourful crocus chase away gloom.
Dazzling daffodils debut in flower,
Welcoming in spring's finest hour.

Mavis Preston-Riley

SUSIE

'Good morning my darling, I'll open the door,
Oh dear! Is it painful that poor little paw?'
I could tell how you hung it, that all was not well
Since your story began with a ring at my bell.
I opened my door and a lady stood there,
She spends her days working in animal care.
'Come and see what I have in the back of my van.'
'Oh no,' I replied 'I don't think that I can.'
For my last little victim of cruelty and pain
Had died, and my efforts had all been in vain.
I had loved her and tended her every need,
But she succumbed to the injury,
Of a cruel human deed.
But nevertheless I crept out in the dark,
And as the door opened, a faint little bark,
A tiny sad creature, so bony and bald,
'Oh! Come here, you poor little darling,' I called,
My heart, it just melted, and I said, 'Come with me,
This home, is now your home, and forever will be.'
I bathed her and fed her and went to the vet,
She is now fit and healthy, a wonderful pet.
We both love each other, a truly loyal friend,
And I thank God that Susie to me He did send.
Now - this happy little Yorkie, is proud as proud can be,
Walking down the road on four legs using only three.

Sylvia D Saunders

HE LOVES ME REALLY

She's here again, that woman of mine,
Doesn't speak, she hasn't the time.
She's busy dragging the hoover out,
'Plug it in pet' I hear her shout.
There's washing strewn all over the floor,
I'd give her a lift, but my back's still sore.
She's upstairs now changing the bed,
I wish she'd stop, she's doing my head.
She's in and out like a deranged bat,
There's one thing for sure, she'll never be fat.
The ironing all neatly folded in a pile,
'That's that done!' She says with a smile.
Off to school to pick up our son,
Ah! A woman's work is never done.
I think I'll go and peel her some spuds,
On second thoughts, I'll shower and change my duds.
'Tea's ready! It's on the table,
Get out the knives and forks if you're able.'
Oh! She's stopped now rushing around,
Emmerdale on so don't make a sound.
It's nine o'clock, time for a brew,
'You make it love while I go to the loo.'
'Go to bed dear, I won't be a minute,
It'll just be warm by the time I get in it.'
I climb into bed, she's asleep already,
I love her really cause she's better than me teddy.

Linda Woodhouse

The Dilemma

I used to own a half an acre,
A meadow, lush and sweetly grassed,
And a tree, a noble tree
Which artists viewed with itching palms.
And then, to take advantage of the grass,
A horse. Retired, his only job
To keep the grass a tidy length.
But soon I found this horse of mine
Was nibbling at the lower limbs
Of my fine tree. Which, for a start
Upset the tree's brave symmetry.
But what, I asked myself, is going to be
The effect upon the horse? Can he
Digest the substance of my tree?
And does he know which trees are good
To eat and - more important - which are not?
And does my duty lie with horse
Or tree? Which to protect from which?
They settled this without my help.
Cold weather killed both horse and tree.
And my lush grass - the council took the land
And swamped it with a new estate
Of council houses. Artists turned the other way.

Bill Johnson

NETHER BOWER

Sit me in a chair at Nether Bower
where the sun sets on Long Sleddale
and I'll hear the cuckoo call the evening hour
while clouds in turmoil on Goat Scar
tumble o'er the rim
dragging the sack of night
heavy with stars.

Peace will be ours at Nether Bower
when the earth is warm on Long Sleddale
and the massing rooks defy the buzzard's power
while clouds in white confusion writhe
a mile above Sadgill
cloaking Buckbarrow Crag
promising rain.

Be by my side at Nether Bower
and walk the old ways of Long Sleddale
we'll search the woods for the rarest flower
while clouds which shadow Harter Fell
become a childhood game
of pictures in the sky
for us to guess.

Sleep in my arms at Nether Bower
when Lakeland night has filled Long Sleddale
and the owl is the watchman in the silent tower
while clouds which glide across the moon
imitate our embrace
then quickly part
before her gaze.

G E Sowerby

THE FREEDOM OF SOLITUDE

I thought I'd lost it,
That edge,
The willingness to push my limits,
To seek out the high and wild places.

I thought I'd settled for,
The easy life,
The relaxed meals with a glass of port,
Followed by gentle strolls with the dog.

But now, imprisoned,
By duty,
With the mountains shouting from the clear horizon,
I crave the freedom of solitude.

Ray Pilling

LARA

Lara -
    wrapped
        in tea towel
   sits
      hawk-eyed
                on mummy's lap
      looks
         at lumps
           of thick red
               paint
    mash
       in her hands
   splat
     on white
        paper
            making marks
       in Daddy's
         head.

Seth Wilkins

TIME SLIPS BY

When all your hopes and dreams are gone
And time is running out
You wonder how the time has passed
So quickly down the spout

Have I wasted all this time
You've asked yourself before
What will I do, with what I've left
Now time means so much more

Every hour is precious, to you now
No time to scream and shout
You savour every minute you have
'Cos' every second counts

I'll put pen to paper, and write it all down
And plan for the time ahead
I'll say to myself, 'Now get off your butt'
And do something constructive instead

It's funny how, when you realise
How time has slipped you by
Because time! It waits for no man
And time! You cannot buy

So treasure every moment you have
From the cradle, to the grave
Waste no time at all, and when you are old
Look back on the time, that you've saved

Mighty Mouse

STONES

Stones can be obstacles
That make us feel blue,
Or just gentle stepping stones
To broaden our view.

Stones can be rolling
And gather no moss,
Or set in a graveyard
Through some poignant loss.

Stones can be pebbles
We find on the beach,
And stones can be found
In a plum or a peach.

And some are the cornerstones
Of buildings we love,
And they fill us with warmth
In some favourite alcove.

And the rocks that we climb
To get to the top,
Will crumble with time
And downwards they'll drop.

But the hard stones, the soft stones
They're all there together,
Creating the landscape
In all kinds of weather.

But some stones are abstract
Historical archives,
The milestones we pass through
Till the end of our lives.

And some stones are sculptured
To a famous man's bust,
But in the end like us all
Will crumble to dust.

Frances Etheridge

Loss

Why didn't the sun fall from the sky
The day you left this world for the next?
Why no sudden pain, no sense of loss?
Why did the sun still shine?
Why did the birds so sweetly sing
When they must have known that you were gone?
Now I'm alone without your love, and never even said goodbye.

Lily Jeffries

My Memory

What did you do with your talents?
Have you asked yourself today?
Did you hide them in your cupboard?
Did you bring them out to play?
Did you say that special 'Thank you'?
You know you said you would
It's no good feeling guilty
You're that one - you know you said you could
You meant to put that patch on
But it's still lying in the drawer
A stitch in time you tell us
You've dropped one on the floor
Did you collect your neighbour's shopping?
No trouble at all - you said
Why did you forget that promise?
Did you stay too long in bed?
God gave us many talents
Perhaps to bake, and sing or sew
He tries to remind you daily
But do you remember - alas no!

Edna A M Cattermole

THE FACES OF NIAGARA

Time worshipped its beauty
With the approval of God
And introduced a magnificence no mortal could mock
The glory of the seasons
Share a valuable host
And the faces of Niagara appear on their clock

Came the face of creation
In league with the spring
And baptises the tulips at nature's request
And the yellow seas of daffodils
Amount a tidal response
Flooding all eyes with beauty as a seasonal guest

Came the face of happiness
Asking summer to stay
To spread the invasion of its sabbatical genes
Ferrying the scent and commitment
Of its floral displays
Across a plush green fertility of picturesque dreams

Came the face of contentment
When autumn finally arrives
Submitting the orders that the trees must obey
Green, yellow and orange
And red leaves will live
Reflecting the sunlight before the fall of the day

Came the face of wonderment
Providing winter with wealth
Spraying ice from the falls upon the surrounding decor
Lamp posts and trees
Are frozen and blessed
Like architectural art work on a glacial shore

And those who pay homage
Shall witness and praise
And bathe in the beauty their presence expects
The memories will flourish
And forever visit the mind
Thus the faces of Niagara commission this eternal respect

David Bridgewater

Fighting Alone

I can't suffer in silence any more,
Rotting my soul down to its core,
I'm being engulfed by myself,
My own worst enemy, no one else.

Suffocating alone in my mind,
Never relenting, never kind,
A part of me is not my friend,
Struggling to bring it to an end.

I'm out of control and afraid,
Trapped in a void full of decay,
I just can't pull myself together,
My inner world is lost forever.

Fighting to breathe, to carry on,
A battle to win with myself,
Confusion and fear mixed within,
Crying with painful memories in.

Sorting out my every thought,
Making myself more distraught,
My shoulders sagging with the strain,
Will I ever end this pain?

Angela Taylor

CLOUDS

My first stories
drifting away on aerial winds,
shape-shifting as I gaze
from Viking ship to dragon,
endless realms,
human faces, animal forms.

Ephemeral structures,
sometimes frightening,
heavy, dark, dangerous
hiding the sun,
or a magic, glowing
circle round the moon.

Floating in the air,
symbol of another place
beyond our reach.
Yet, by a paradox,
defining our world
when viewed from space.

C A Browne

MR RIGHT

He must be tall
And handsome too,
With jet black hair
And eyes of blue.

A luxury car
And penthouse flat.
I could be satisfied
With that.

Restaurants only
Of the best.
At least 5 star,
Forget the rest.

A lady of leisure
I would be.
I'd shop, do lunch,
Have friends for tea.

He'd pamper me,
And come what may,
Remember birthdays
And Valentine's Day.

My Mr Right
Would perfect be
And loyal and true
For all to see.

I must be honest
And stop dreaming -
I'll take any man
As long as he's breathing!

Mary Andersen

THE BATTLE

Many wounds have passed since these men went to war,
onwards and upwards,
bigger weapons than before.
Bogey B took cover,
he shivered on patrol,
the arms' race crazy,
simply way out of control.
Then his friend threw it,
the latest device,
Bogey B went and got it,
against all advice.
His leg was split,
his energy lost,
how many more will this dreaded war cost?
Then came the bombs,
and the disease tumbling down,
if the bug didn't get you,
you probably drowned.
But the men fought on through hunger and pain,
fighting to live a normal life again.
So fight for Bogey B,
and with him his friend,
but fight with honour,
fight until the end.

Adam Kennedy (13)

It's So Quiet . . .

It's so quiet without you,
wish you were here right now,
sat down beside me,
but that is the way things are,

We had so much fun when we were young,
we still have things to learn;
about the world around us,
the people we love and care,

I remember the day you left us,
the day we all stood and sobbed,
we are so many miles apart now,
but it does not stop our love,

I will always remember our loving days,
until my days stop.

Julie Ann Garritty (16)

THE WOODSMAN

Distant eyes the colour of November
Quiet strength sinews broad back and arm
Hard work shuts out the hurt, the need to remember
Silent woods act as a salve, soothe wounds like balm

His limbs are as oak limbs, sturdy and polished brown
His heartwood age-ring banded, each ring a separate pain
A gentle fierce-natured man that life damaged, let down
Healing himself in his dark green world, witnessed only by
                                        the trees and soft rain

Sarah Kaye Martin

My Child Quietly Sleeps

Shaky, frail branches, crying out for help,
They take over, surround, all nature so bitter,
The frosty bite, a chillingly realistic sight,
Visions of warmth by healing, welcoming fires,
What nature, I enjoy, yet destroy.
The cruelty inflicted, all our tyrannous spite.

The way I ran, walked, talked, explored,
The paths of freedom, straight and narrow,
My child quietly sleeps; me, I solemnly adored,
My child now weeps, but his ghost is restored.
As all comes tumbling down, my mind can still rest,
My child may have fallen but he'll rise to the test.

The grass is dying, it's been worn down, abused,
As it tells its own priceless tale,
My future collides with everyone else's past.
My cauldron of hate, threatens to boil over,
It's blowing a hole, cutting through my insides,
My child's spirit, it must live at last.

My child quietly sleeps. He; I solemnly adored,
My child now wilts and weeps, but his ghost is restored.

The trees, now sprouting new growth,
New life awakens, as one life is left torn at the seams.
As the broken shedded bark, litters the damp, infested ground,
The marshy earth, leads to fields of gold,
The footprints, now restored, although dead waste looms,
My child has been here, his spirit profound.

Where did he go?
Why can't he see me so?
Is it still his time to hide?
Or can I never turn the tide?

Simon Cardy

ALBERT THE ELF

Albert the elf lived in the wood
Under a toadstool, as all elves should
With his wife and children three,
All as happy as could be.

In the evening as darkness fell
The wood came alive, in Dingly Dell
All the family came out to play
And Albert his whistle began to play.

As he played, the children danced
Round and round, the woods, they pranced
Mother sang without a care
Magical music everywhere.

Then as quickly as they came,
The music ceased, silence fell again,
The sun was rising in Dingly Dell,
Arriving with the dawn, it had broken the spell.

Perhaps if we crept back tonight,
We may behold a similar sight
If we are quiet, you never know,
Albert may repeat the show.

S M Rooney

MOTHER

There she works without a stop,
If not dishes, it's a pot,
Whilst we go out and have our fun,
Mother's work is never done.

She tries to give us all the same,
Helps us keep an honest name,
Sometimes she seems so cross and curt,
But that's to shelter us from hurt.

Why should we not to Mother give,
A little thought that she might live
To mingle with us now and then,
And make her life worthwhile again.

So let us brush away today,
The selfish thought the angry way,
For when she's gone for evermore,
We'll miss her then, if not before.

Jock Milne

SUB CONSCIENCE

Stop!
Or shall I do this?
Or shall I do that?
It's all very much a matter of
Fact.
Shall I do things that I like best
And to hell with the rest?
Or shall I do nothing at all.

What if I do that and don't
Like it
And find out I'd rather do this?
What if I do this and don't like it?
It has to be hit or I'll miss.

Should I just please other people
And not bother so much about me?
Or should I jump in at the deep end
And swim very far out to sea?

My mind is in turmoil and quandary
I really don't know what to do
Do the best for yourself
Sod everyone else!
After all life belongs just to you.

Thought
Don't always do as others
Tell you.

Brenda Nicholson

SHADOWS

Flickering shadows on a firelit wall,
Advance, retreat, grow, fade, move constantly.
Dreams dance with shadows, waver, rise and fall,
Merge and are lost in poignant memory.

Hazel Wellings

FEAR RUBS MY SENSES

I can hear cries of suffering and pain,
From tortured people, helpless animals, appalling cruelty so inhumane.
Oceans full with tears shed,
Coloured with their blood so red;
Their butchered hearts no longer throb,
Upon the scarlet waves they bob.

Rotting flesh I can smell
From sinew and muscle, carcass and shell;
Obnoxious odours so intense,
My nostrils sharply they incense.

Against my skin I feel cold flesh and bones,
Numbing my body are skeletons and horns.
Meadows strewn with fur and feathers
Freely blowing amongst the heathers;
Butchered hearts upon scarlet waves,
Oh, the dreadful way that man behaves.

Like detecting in wine a certain grape,
On my tongue I taste mankind's rape;
Blood and sinew feed the vine,
Fermenting in an acid wine.
It fills me with horror what cruelty entails,
I see gorged out eyes and mangled entrails.

Martin Howard

FREEDOM TO ROAM

Over hills and streams
And barbed wire fences,
Across fields blanketed with sheep
Smelling the flowers, lulled into sleep,
These carefree days
Sharpen the senses
The cows wait to greet the dawn
The red sky sends out a warning.

The patter of rain on the leaves
And whispering voices of the trees.
In this haunted wood
There is nothing to fear,
It is the spirit of nature
Drawing near,
The silence pervades all
Every nook and cranny
Every farmyard wall.

I feel safe in nature's arms
I respect the environment
And leave it as I found it
I will do nature no harm,
I just want to roam the land
Take mother nature by the hand,
Freedom is the song I sing
But freedom with responsibility.

The freedom to roam
This habitat is my home,
A wind carried song
I will do nature no wrong.

Ian Barton

The New Millennium

The new millennium now is due,
It means so much to me and to you.
The greatest prophet in a stable born,
Bringing forth a wonderful new dawn.

Thus emerged the Christian teaching.
Of love, tolerance and justice far reaching.
From the Holy Child to a prophet of love,
Created by the loving God from above.

This spiritual prophet, 'twas Jesus by name,
By spiritual conception through Mary he came.
Bringing together all religions in unity,
But religious intolerance did not bring immunity.

Plotting and scheming bigotry, started to grow,
Jesus' prophecy commenced to show.
He knew his physical death had been foretold,
Despite all his teachings, more precious than gold.

His cruel death did not stop the good news,
Though there are many religions all with different views.
Religious intolerance brought forth terrorism and strife,
This cannot be God's plan, that created Jesus and all human life.

Robert Baslington

Kirstie's Song

Changing colours in my world,
Forever fresh and new,
Tiny hands brush my face,
Like the touch of morning dew,
Dancing spirit like the wind,
Smiles with a starry sky,
The smell of rosebud skin,
Bright and fragile butterfly,
Little girl to let you know,
Your mummy's watching as you grow.

Gentle footsteps in the sand,
Creep softly through the night,
Beats a heart of purest gold,
Dark eyes that shine with light,
Spoken words on angel wings,
Like seasons as they pass,
Treasures unfold, joys untold,
China doll you break like glass,
My little girl, gift from above,
You mummy thanks you for your love.

Sharon Gardner

BEDSIT LAND

Clock ticking monotonously,
Brainwashing by repetition,
Lonely somnambulistic days embrace the horizon,
Boredom stretches into infinity,
Bedsit land.
Television, breakfast, radio, dinner,
Should I get dressed today?
Maybe tomorrow - if it ever comes,
Post arrives. Gas, electric, water, council tax.
The four horsemen of my apocalypse,
Dishes to be washed, carpets to hoover and shelves to dust,
On the other hand there are talk shows to watch,
Sad individuals airing their horrendous lives for all to judge and feel superior to,
Signing on day tomorrow, last shred of dignity lost,
This means having to leave the security,
The security I have become addicted to -
The depressing four walled existence that is bedsit land!

Donna M Holt

Castle Deceased

The castle stands both bold and proud,
Has done for so many a year.
It's crooked fingers pierce the sky,
Protruding now from broken hands.
Veins of ivy cling to life
Binding masonry that's near,
Wiry, sinuous, flexed by wind,
Feet embedded in barren sand.
Ghostly voices haunt the ear
Invisible to naked eye.
Bleached ribs flicker in the moonlight,
As timber joints do slowly sag.
Neglected, weathered, almost bare.
Doomed to death by nature's hand.
Body of innocence, faces decay
As cataracts of mist descend.
Another corpuscle to break its back,
For structure long ago was skinned.
A skeleton, resting in its shroud.

D J Holt

Forest Fruits

Come with me on a journey
a world far - from ours
no corner shop - no ready supplies
survival - is the name of the game
to a place dark and mysterious
a place not to venture alone
stop - look around - hear every sound
food is here in plenty - on bush-tree-ground
a careful balance - always maintained
scattered scraps - by foresters - we trust
predators - stoats - weasels - man - take care we must
squirrels - mice - vole
hurry now to bury seeds - nuts
winter's cache - a harvest for all
just beyond the canopy
a swift - silent woodland owl flies
fieldfare - redwing - buntings - thrushes and tits
dine on - how spindle - stone - bramble or hips
protected in hawthorn hedges, until winter is past
some hibernate - away from harsh winds and snow
awaits the arrival of warm spring air
a strange place maybe - but -
it's our place to care

David Charles

ON REFLECTION

Hold back the days
Where have they all gone,
Hold back the days
They say life goes on.

Hold back the years
They pass too fast,
Hold back the tears
They're now in the past.

Be still for awhile
And then we will see,
What has to be
Surely will be.

We'll get where we are going
So what's all the rush,
When we come to the end
We won't need a push.

Kathleen Leigh

FOR CARLO THE CAVALIER

He is gone,
My friend of many years.
His devotion,
The expressions and funny ways,
His companionship.

Is it a better place?
I hope it is for him.
I am left in devastation,
Although his years were many,
One wanted more of them.

He is gone,
Many memories left of him.
In my mind,
Still seen and heard, his funny ways.
His voice, the expressions on his face.

The end was so sudden.
Barely two weeks wondering why.
What was wrong, was there pain?
His trusting eyes, his soft fur.
Now his spirit wanders the hills of Rossendale.

He is gone,
Sad thoughts but many pleasant memories.
His ashes scattered in the hills
Where he first lived and played,
No longer in body, but always in spirit,
Memories of him.

David F Upson

PIG WIGGY

Gradely face
A sparkling eye
Two pink ears
A snout to pry
Troughing in your little sty
My piggy
A happy mouth of toothless grace
Table manners . . . lost to haste
And swallowed charm . . . for nought to waste
Pig wiggy
Your grovelled grunts
Ecstatic squeal
Enraptured over swill and peel
So clumsily my heart you steal
Dear piggy
O little pig come sing to me
Come roll about upon my knee
For evermore my love will be
For you my Pig Wig Wiggy.

Olwyn Kershaw

LOVE IS IN THE AIR 2000

Romance goes back to ancient times
When 15th February, was the date to dine,
A Fertility Festival to celebrate
The date when all birds, began to mate,
But later in the 1800s, cards began to sell,
Elaborate printed cards, written poems as well.
Nowadays it's humorous tones, funny, and rude,
Instead of romantic prose, cards are really crude.
Saucy cards declaring more basic feelings,
Instead of sensitive romance, that's really appealing.
Once written . . . 'Valentine you are . . .
Everything that I worship from afar,
It's your loving that I really want,
So please use a better deodorant,
Though I hold you, in highest regard,
When you tuck yourself in and think you're thin,
You resemble a barrel of lard'.

Woe betide the guy who wrote this,
It certainly puts stop to a lover's kiss!
This is not secret, and unrequited love,
Romantic flowers for your turtle dove,
Diamonds are still, a girl's best friend,
If you can't afford jewels, then a rose do send.
On February 14th 2000, love is again in the air,
A setting sun, sets the scene, with romantic flare.
The romance of the 'new millennium' I see,
Men all over the world, get down on one knee,
Soaring up on a balloon flight above,
Please will you be my 'leap year love'?
Only if you're up for it darling!

Brenda R Matthews

A Poem/Song About Insomnia

It's a fine line between a genius and a madman,
Just a stone's throw away from the beach.
That's what they say in the ads man
But the truth is a long way to reach.

Chorus
Oh I wish I could sleep in my big fancy bed
But the thoughts go around and around in my head
So it's off to the chemical cosmos instead
Goodnight and God bless you all!

They say an apple a day keeps the doctor away
But I'm not so sure these days.
I don't know about God but I promise and pray
For a rest from my cranial maze.

Chorus

So it goes every day full of anguish and pain
As the illness runs riot I begin.
In the dark still of night I am driven insane
By the thoughts in the maelstrom within.

Chorus

Anthony Cohen

THE TALL SHIPS

The tall ships are gone from the ports of the world.
Gone from the seven seas.
Rolling along with sails unfurled.
We shall not see their like again.

Sailing the trade routes of the sea
With bales of cotton in their holds.
Cargoes of grain and wool and tea,
To-ing and fro-ing across the globe.

Montevideo and far Bombay.
The China and Australia run.
Biscuits and salt beef day after day.
Poor fare for tough, hard drinking men.

A shipwright's eye and pride and will
Built the ships of seasoned oak.
Shaping the timbers with craftsman's skill
The ships are gone but the sea remains.

D H Taylor

E FROW 1906-1997

Edmund Eddie Frow
Wasn't born of Salford, you know.

He fought for the working class.
In Salford, for every unemployed, lad and lass.
Socialist pride he'd never hide.
A union man, he brought change.
British rights,
In every worker's sight.
Bosses cruel might put to flight.
In grey areas, we now see light.
Thankfully he gave for fellow man/woman.
Working class movement library was, his given pride.
Organised, run with his wife.
Ruth, always by his side.
Eddie, labour foundations you laid well.
Socialist principles he would never lose, sell.
Eddie, for many you were a good guide.
A terrible loss to mankind, when you died.

H Livesey

My First Grandchild

What shall we call thee baby fine
We shall call thee love
Oh she who all our worlds entwine
What shall we call thee

What shall we call thee baby fine
We shall call thee hope
Oh love that fills this heart of mine
What shall we call thee

What shall we call thee baby fine
We shall call thee peace
Our life, our love, our hearts are thine
Oh what shall we call thee

What shall we call thee baby fine
We shall call thee blessed
You are a gift and so much more
Oh what shall we call thee

What shall we call thee baby fine
We shall call thee Jasmine Emma.

Richard Wallbank

SHUTTLE SCUTTLE

After crossings by ferry and by plane,
Experiencing the hovercraft, too,
It was about time to try 'Le Shuttle'
Going *under* 'La Manche' was overdue.

Whilst not knowing just what to expect,
'Midst warnings of strikes at both ends
'Twas with some trepidation we booked
Despite those strange looks from our friends.

We left at a quarter to midnight
Admitting that sleep would be rare,
A coachload of duty free seekers,
City Europe would soon be laid bare.

We were in the queue by six-thirty
To enter a tube-like chasm.
'If you see any fish, shout out loud'
Said our driver, oozing sarcasm.

Canned greetings welcomed us all on board.
In minutes we were shooting through,
But apart from a slight rocking motion
There was no sense of speed down this flue.

Thirty-five minutes is the schedule,
You can stay put or wander around.
If you fancy a trip on the shuttle
It's good value, ten francs to the pound.

Roy Gordon

SILENCE

Silence is all around here,
Something I never had before,
Which makes me lock the door.
And yet,
The stream talks its way
Over stones.
No, not time for bed yet.
The stars light up the sky,
No orange street lamps
Hide their glory.
Is that an owl in that old tree?
I'll just turn out the light
Then maybe I can see.

What can I hear in the
Quiet of the night?
A dog barks, over at the farm.
I hear an aeroplane
Heading off, in a night time sky.
Is that cry across the valley
The sound of a peacock?
Not so quiet here.
Sounds I never heard before
Comfort me through my locked door.

Carole Anne Weaver

My Misunderstood Husband

My husband is always misunderstood,
He has a side people fail to see,
They see a man who only stirs fear,
But things are very different for me.

Nobody seems to understand,
Why I love such a violent man,
But despite all the pain he causes,
Love him I certainly can.

He might cause pain and unpleasant things,
To me he's loving and gentle,
But people who often go to him,
Think he's unstable or mental.

Whenever I pay him a visit at work,
I walk up to his door,
From outside I hear the sound of pain,
As his victims shriek once more.

Even walking down the street,
People look, whisper and glare,
'That's the woman who's married to him,
How can *he* love or care?'

He never wants to hurt anyone,
I wish they'd all get the gist,
That my husband is really a loving man,
Despite being the local dentist.

Helen McEvoy

AGELESS

Age is a state of mind they say
And this is very true
Because your youth has been and gone
It's not the end of you
These years are meant to be for you
To do the things you wanted to
This seemed impossible before
Age had taken wings
Now you've earned the right to choose
What you do each day
It doesn't matter about your age
Or what some people say
This time is yours and yours alone
To do the best you can
Don't be a lonely 'stay at home'
Enjoy your full life's span
Believe you are just starting out
On some great holiday
But never, never think you are old
You'll give the game away.

C Allison

LOST FRIENDS

I walk the country lane we knew,
Though now, I'm on my own.
For the one whose hand I held, as we walked,
Is sadly, no more at home.
He died on a beach, over there in France.
On a beach, with a familiar name.
Though, as time has passed, I cannot recall,
Whether it was 'Juno' or 'Gold', they were much the same.

His Collie Ross, used to lie in wait for him,
Behind the door each day.
In the hope his friend would come to take him,
For a walk, down what we once called our lane.
Then as the sun, it started to set,
He'd come nudge my hand with his nose,
And gaze at me with his beautiful eyes,
From which the love he felt, seemed to flow.

It was as though he was trying to say to me,
Why hasn't my friend come home again.
I've waited for him another day, and
It's so hard to stand the pain.
One day, Ross must have decided,
He'd suffered the pain for too long,
As he lay on his side, he gave a great sigh,
And so quickly, from me was gone.

Now as I walk our lane alone,
I'll sometimes sit amidst the heather,
To console myself, with but one thought,
My lost friends are now together.

Joseph Yates

ALEC ANONYMOUS

Alec Anonymous
is not well known
Alec Anonymous
lives at home all alone
Alec Anonymous
has no friends on this earth
Alec Anonymous
has known no one since birth
Alec Anonymous
is so lonely and blue
when you enquire about Alec
the response you receive will be 'Who?'

Jake

THE COVERING LETTER

To
my to, your from
whomever
not merely whom, mind you
but ever
it may
a politeness, a percentage
and finally, a prayer
concern.

Please
my plea, your displeasure
find enclosed
which is little to ask
in light of what follows
this,
for your pleasure
your undivided judgement
your percentage gain.

Yours
unequivocally, patently,
uniquely with no doubt
faithfully,
as a servant
as a lover
a believer
as a dog
an unfamiliar, uninvited
unprepossessingly emaciated
Dog.

Dale Overton

SPARKLE AND GLOW

Hallowe'en, Trick or Treat has passed
Bonfire beacons in the night,
Guy Fawkes is burning well to everyone's delight.
Be safe to see the display - so grand
Beacons all over this land
The sparkle and the rockets
Don't carry fireworks or matches in your pockets.
Keep your dogs and cats in, don't burn the hedgehog,
Mind the whistling rockets and the burning log.

Enjoy the Roman candles, Catherine wheel and volcano
Cascades of stars, sparkle and all the glow.
Have baked potato, chestnuts, hot drinks and soup
Stand around with neighbours and your family group
By now dark rings around your eyes, clothes smell of smoke
Throw extra wood or have a final stoke.

Next morning smouldering ashes,
You cough at the smoke.
Let off your last firework
Like you had just begun
Remembering last night here,
All safe and fun.

F Williamson

OUR COUNTY

It isn't always holiday time
  In this county of the red rose,
But there are many holiday towns here
  Where visitors come and go.

Blackpool, is the most known
  With its tower so upright and grand.
Entertainment is its main source,
  Overlooking sea and sand.

Further south is St Anne's-on-Sea
  And Lytham, with its windmill and green.
Look over the Ribble Estuary,
  Southport, can be seen.

Go inland to the many big towns,
  Shop in the well-known stores.
Preston, Manchester, Bury and Blackburn
  Have arcades, by the score.

Rochdale, the home of the late Gracie Fields
  And the first Co-operative so grand.
A town hall, that stands, facing the hills,
  With a park, and a lake, near at hand.

Bolton, Wigan, and Chorley are there,
  All jewels in Lancashire's crown.
Ribchester, on the River Ribble,
  Where the Romans settled down.

There is so much to see in this county.
  Amusement parks, castles and halls.
The countryside, a patchwork of greenery,
  And caverns, canals, caves and waterfalls.

If you visit this red rose county,
  Think of the things you can see.
God made this beautiful county
  And left it for you and for me.

Joan Smith

LIFE'S PATHWAY

This letter is to wish you well in your life
think about what you do,
it will show what type of person you are.
Be kind to others
they will be kind to you.
In this life you get back
what you put into it.
Take care, choose friends with thought,
enjoy life and all it has to offer,
be true to yourself
be content
as always there will be others
who will seem better than yourself.
You are you and not them.
Be a first you
and not copy of someone else.
When life gets hard
as it will,
your family will be there for you.
They may wonder at some of the things you'll do
but they will still love you, their child.
May these words help you
along the pathway of life.

Lynda Banks

The Morning Walk

I smell the salt in the grey stormy waves
As they crash on the chalky ledge
I smell the fish that have blown ashore
And who now thrash about on the edge

As I walk along, the lavender smell
From the gardens each side of the lane
Reaches my nostrils, as does the grass
New mown and still wet from the rain

I reach the café, no tourists are there
It's early. They are all still in bed
But the smell of fresh coffee draws me near
Though I may have the chocolate instead

There is no better way to start the day
And I'm lured by the smell of fresh toast
But there's no better smell than fresh morning air
On my walk, that's the smell I love most

Anne Patricia Jones

TOTALLY TEMPERANCE

Those lonely men who frequent bars
Shouldn't take along their cars
The police don't mind who was in it
Unless they've imbibed over the limit
They make you blow into a plastic bag
Like some Jape or university rag
If you fail the breathalyser test
No doubt the police will do the rest
The magistrate has not proposed what you hoped
Now your licence has been revoked
Next time leave your car parked in your drive
Don't you want to live and stay alive?
Another time you may bee more aware
You just have to take a little bit of care
It may mean an epitaph as a remembrance
It's better to stay sober and totally temperance

Francis Arthur Rawlinson

SUNDAYS ON LADY STREET

Children belt footballs against the walls,
squabbling vehemently about the verdict,
scolded brusquely by irate parents.

Radios crackle through open doorways,
Billy Cotton bellowing 'Wakey, wakey,'
Guy Mitchell 'Singing The Blues'.

Cycle spokes rotate robustly,
spinning clockwise in dazzling sunlight,
methodically preserved for the week ahead.

Men return from dinner time drinking,
laughing, joking, talking loudly,
hotly disputing yesterday's sport.

Pigeons scowl from tiled rooftops,
vigilant eyes always watchful,
hovering for morsels, spying for food.

Chattering neighbours pow wow on doorsteps,
bartering scandal from Sunday weeklies,
gleaning gossip for their next encounter.

Paul Kelly

The Raging Sea

In storm and tempest hear our plea,
Protect us from the raging sea,
When storm clouds gather, in howling gales,
When mighty waves, break o'er ships' rails.

The fearful might, the roar of thunder,
Those wrathful waves, that send ships under.
For some great ships, that man has made,
No match against that great tirade.

Nor less at risk, those on the shore,
The futile barriers, o'er which waves roar.
Yet, witnessing this rage and thunder,
Of nature's might, a thing of wonder.

Through this dark and raging nigh,
The blessed dawn, brings calm and light.
For when the mighty roars do cease,
As if by magic, comes calm and peace.

Eddie Preston

SUBMISSIONS INVITED
SOMETHING FOR EVERYONE

POETRY NOW 2000 - Any subject, any style, any time.

WOMENSWORDS 2000 - Strictly women, have your say the female way!

STRONGWORDS 2000 - Warning! Age restriction, must be between 16-24, opinionated and have strong views. (Not for the faint-hearted)

All poems no longer than 30 lines. Always welcome! No fee! Cash Prizes to be won!

Mark your envelope (eg *Poetry Now*) **2000**
Send to:
Forward Press Ltd
Remus House, Coltsfoot Drive,
Woodston,
Peterborough, PE2 9JX

OVER £10,000 POETRY PRIZES TO BE WON!

Judging will take place in October 2000